AF470829

How to run the BUSES

This series, of general reading interest, also has an eye on careers. It explains how service industries, in contrast to manufacturing industries, are run. Each is concerned with an activity that touches the lives of most people, and which employs many thousands of workers. Here are explained the 'secrets' of success in one service; how the complex web of movement and activity reaches the public at many points. How does a plane land safely in a storm? How does a railway, with merely a three-minute train interval, avoid smash-ups?

Titles in this series:

How to run an AIRPORT
How to run a RAILWAY
How to run the BUSES
How to run a CHAIN STORE

All of these books are reliable and up to date, have been vetted by experts in their trades, are written in lively, narrative and participant fashion, and contain many pages of plates. Where necessary careers guides and glossaries have been added.

General editor: Sally Brooks

For books about the manufacturing industries please see the IT'S MADE LIKE THIS BOOKS, published by John Baker.

How to run the
BUSES

John Hibbs

JOHN BAKER LONDON

Published in 1972 by
JOHN BAKER (PUBLISHERS) LTD
4, 5 and 6 Soho Square
London W1V 6AD

ISBN 0 212 98409 8

Printed in Great Britain by
THE MILLBROOK PRESS LTD, SOUTHAMPTON

Contents

Acknowledgements

The author and publisher would like to thank the following for permission to reproduce their photographs in this book: Mr R. N. Collins, plate 6; London Transport Executive, plate 2; Mr T. W. Moore, plate 1; National Bus Company, plates 3–5, 7–19.

Author's note

I am greatly indebted to Mr T. M. Glass of the National Bus Company for encouragement in this project, and for helping me to avoid one or two errors of statement, as well as for providing a most valuable selection of prints. I need hardly add that all responsibility for accuracy and interpretation remains stubbornly my own. Without the help of Mr E. Axten, however, in preparing the maps and diagrams, the book would have been far more difficult to understand. I would like finally to record my thanks to the late Mr John Baker for suggesting that I should write the book in the first place.

Illustrations

PLATES

FIGURES IN THE TEXT

CHAPTER 1

Who owns the buses?

Buses are things we are all familiar with. If you think of a busy road and the traffic on it, there's pretty sure to be a bus in the picture. True, you may not be certain whether to call it a bus or a coach, because the two words can mean much the same thing sometimes, which is why the law has to use a special word. A vehicle that you pay to ride in, if it is bigger than a taxi, is officially called a 'public service vehicle', and the person or company or council that runs it is called a public service vehicle operator. Some of these operators are very large concerns, while others are small family businesses; taken all together, they provide a service to the public that many millions of people depend upon to get to and from work, or to go on holiday, or for shopping or visiting – to say nothing of getting to and from school, or going on school outings.

There have been buses on our roads for a good while now, and before the motor bus was invented there were horse buses. For a time there were trams too, but almost everywhere in Britain the buses have taken their place. So the business of running a fleet of buses or coaches has a long tradition behind it, and while there is always something new to learn about the way to do it, it is by now pretty well understood, and it is possible to train to become a manager in the bus industry, just as you might train to become manager of a steel works or a shipping line. Managing a bus fleet is an important job, with a lot more to it than just knowing how the vehicles work (although the industry needs first-rate engineers to see that the buses run safely and economically). Finding out what people want and how much they are prepared to pay for it, and seeing that they get a satisfactory service, keeps the traffic department busy; drivers and conductors have to be trained; records have to be kept and the money has to be accounted for; timetables have to be printed and services have to be advertised so that the public know where and when they can use the buses. In a small firm, one man may well be responsible for almost all of this, while in a large one there will be special managers for different parts of the job.

If you have travelled about Britain, you may have noticed that in different parts of the country there are buses of different colours and with different names on the sides that provide the main services (the names, by the way, are called 'fleet names'). Usually there will be one fleet that you see pretty well all the time, along with others that you don't see so often. Sometimes there will be different buses providing town services from those that run out into the country. Often the school buses will be different again, and so will the coaches that take people on outings to the seaside. So let us first look at the way the industry is organised, so that we can understand better what is going on around us.

There are rather more than 5,000 bus and coach operators in Great Britain. Of these, the State owns nearly seventy, but since they are mainly big ones, they account for over half of the actual vehicles. The great majority are small firms, who together own over a quarter, while a small number of operators are local councils, who own less than a quarter of the vehicles. Figure 1 will make this clearer.

In Chapter 3 we shall see that there are different kinds of service, and in practice an operator will usually stick to one or another type of operation, although there are important exceptions. The State-owned (or nationalised) ones run mostly regular bus services and many of the long-distance services, while the private firms specialise in letting coaches for hire – in some parts of the country they are the only ones that provide school services. The city councils not surprisingly run services largely within their own boundaries, although even here there are cases where they serve neighbouring towns and villages. But then the big nationalised companies also have coaches you can hire, and some of them run school services, while many of them provide city services where local councils do not run their own buses. Quite a few of the small firms run regular services, occasionally in towns and cities, but more usually in the countryside.

At one end of the industry – the operation of coaches and coach services – there is a link with the travel trade. Coach firms need

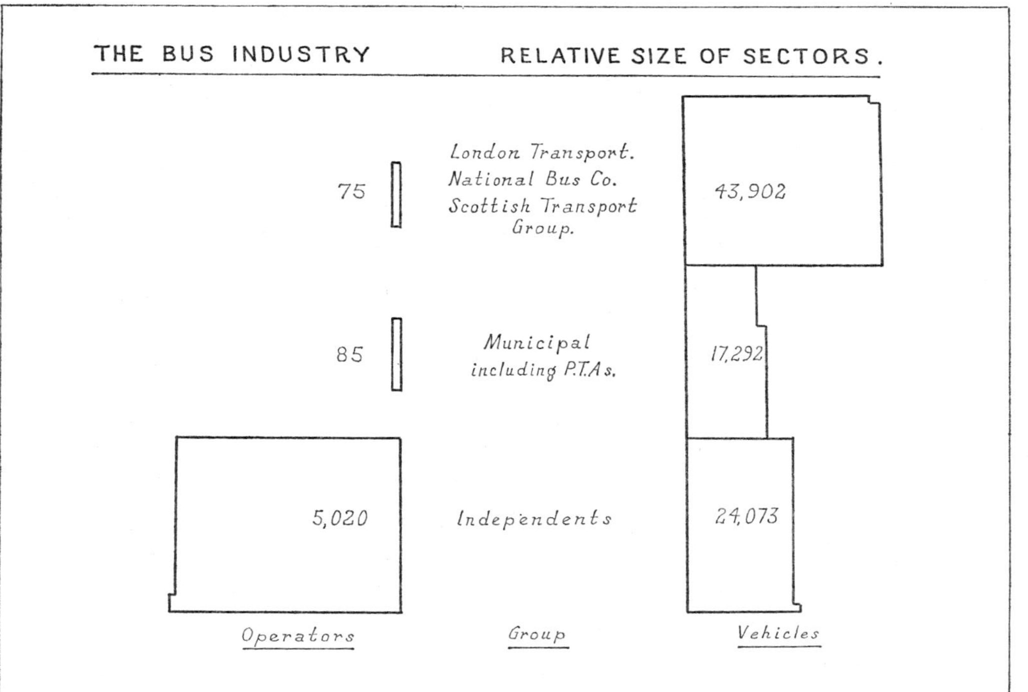

Fig. 1 The main sectors of the industry. The areas in the diagram are proportionate to the number of operators or vehicles in each group

agents to help sell their services, and travel agents often need to hire coaches. Some firms, both private and nationalised, have therefore become involved in this business, and the management of a bus or coach fleet may include responsibility for a travel agent's business as well.

The State-owned companies started as private businesses, and at various times their owners have arranged to sell them to the nation – that is to say, they were never nationalised as a compulsory measure, like the railways were in 1948. Today, these companies are owned, so far as England and Wales are concerned, by the *National Bus Company*, and so far as Scotland is concerned, by the *Scottish Transport Group*. They are the companies with familiar names, well known over wide areas, and a list of them is given at the back of this book. Each of them has its own history, and since each of them has a clearly defined area, or territory, to work in, they are often called the 'territorial companies'. Their names may tell you something about the area they serve, such as *East Kent Road Car Company*, or *Cumberland Motor Services*, but sometimes they have expanded far from their original base, as, for example, *Maidstone & District Motor Services*. A few of them have kept the names of the family that founded the business, as with the *Alexander* companies in Scotland, or the *Crosville* company in the north-west (originally owned by the Crosland Taylor family). In the case of *United Automobile Services*, the title chosen by the founder in 1912 has remained in use right up to the present day. In one special case the fleet name is not even the official title of the company – *Midland Red* buses are owned by the Birmingham & Midland Motor Omnibus Company, which is rather too much of a mouthful to expect people to remember.

If you look carefully at a bus or coach, you can always find out who actually owns it, for the law requires this information to be painted on the side nearest the pavement, and you will find it in small letters down near the ground. Provided the 'legal lettering' is there, a bus does not *have* to have any other name, but the operators like you to know whose vehicle you have been riding in, because they depend upon the 'goodwill' of the public a great deal, which is why the fleet names matter. This is true of the fleets run by town and city councils too, for a lot of local pride can go into a smart fleet of buses carrying, as they often do, the coat of arms of the council concerned.

The organisation of the motor bus industry
The National Bus Company, which as we have seen owns almost all the big bus companies in England and Wales, was set up by Act of Parliament in 1968. This means that it is not like ordinary companies, which are run to make a profit for the people who own shares in them; instead, it is owned by the State (in other words, it is 'nationalised'). But it is called a company because it is expected to behave rather like one, and to use its 'assets' (buses, garages and the like) just as efficiently as if it were an ordinary business concern. There are two reasons that account for its special position as a 'nationalised company'. One is the accident of history which brought much of the industry into State ownership over twenty years ago, by voluntary agreement; the second was the wish of the government in 1968 to make it easier for the bus companies to co-operate with the Passenger Transport Authorities, with the London Transport Executive, and with British Rail.

The NBC (which is what we usually call the National Bus Company) is managed by a board appointed by the Minister of Transport. This then appoints another board, whose members are responsible for the actual running of the companies that the NBC owns – the companies that actually provide the bus and coach services. These companies are themselves arranged in regional groups, with one man in charge of the companies in each group; the groups are shown in figure 2. Thus, from its headquarters in London, the NBC has an organisation that reaches right down to the local bus services in any town or village, and yet, since the individual companies have considerable freedom to take their own decisions, the local service can be managed by someone who knows about local needs. When the NBC was set up, it inherited from the former Transport Holding Company (also a nationalised concern) two big groups of companies. The THC had also been responsible for a third group, operating in Scotland, and this became a separate concern, with a board appointed by the Secretary of State for

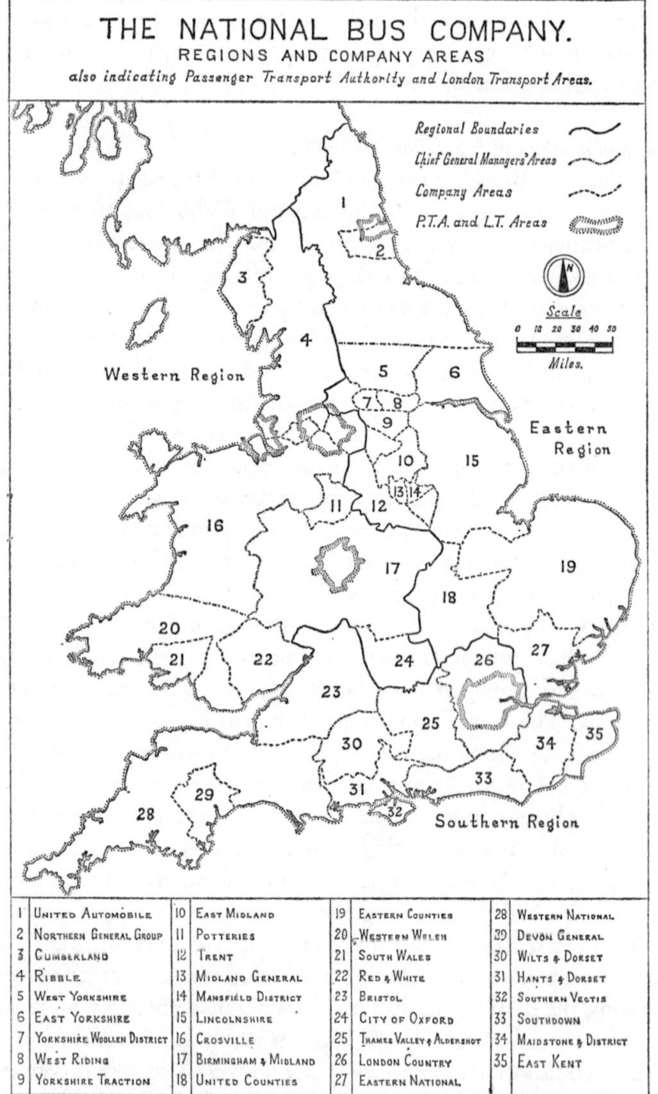

Fig. 2 The geography of bus services in England and Wales. As well as the companies shown, there are some thousands more, but only a fairly small number run public bus services

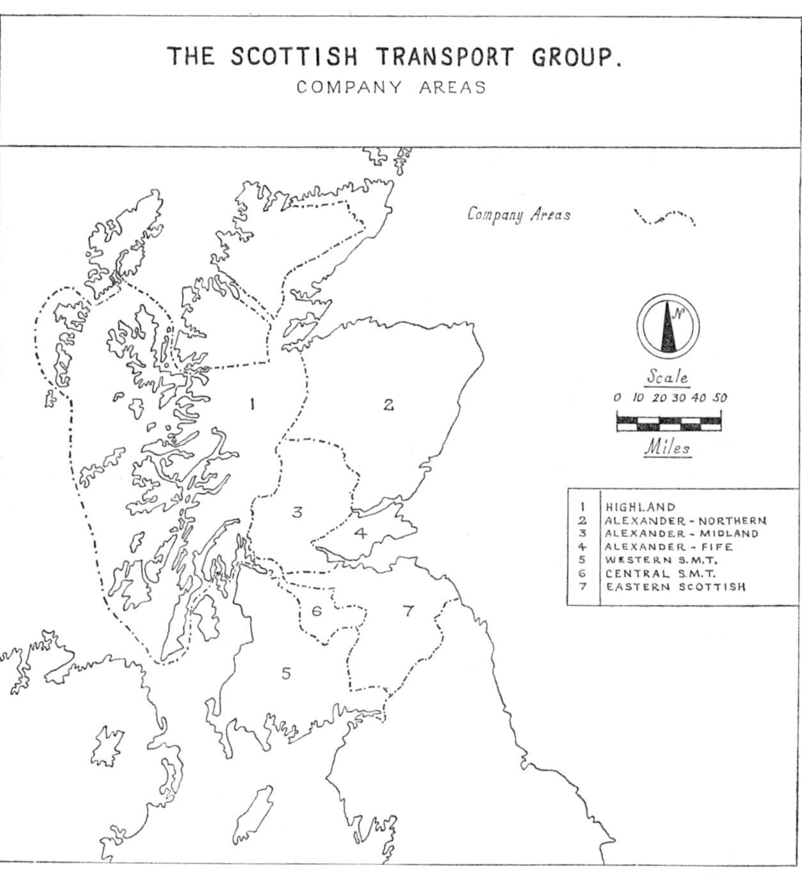

Fig. 3 The geography of bus services in Scotland. Here again there are many more small firms, of which a small number run public bus services

Scotland. Because this group included companies running shipping services, it was called the Scottish Transport Group (STG), but its pattern of organisation is very much the same as that of the NBC. A link exists between the two concerns through the chief executive of each sitting as a member of the board of the other. Figure 3 shows the areas of the STG operating companies.

Another type of transport operator was also set up by the Act of Parliament that formed the NBC and the STG. It was thought that certain parts of the country, where there were a number of borough councils all running their own bus fleets, would get better transport if these fleets were put under one large concern. It was decided to set up an entirely new kind of public body, which is called a Passenger Transport Authority, and four of them have so far been established; for Merseyside, the Manchester area, the Black Country and Tyneside. Each of them consists of people nominated by local councils in the area, together with others appointed by the Minister of Transport, and each of them in turn appoints a Passenger Transport Executive, to do the job of actually running the public services. The intention of Parliament here again was to make it easier for public transport and town planning to be more closely linked, but the final development of the idea will have to wait until the new local government system has been introduced. In the PTA areas, other bus and coach companies (including several that belong to the NBC) continue to exist, and it is not yet clear what arrangements will be made for them to work together with the PTE for the area concerned.

The PTAs have acquired about eighteen bus fleets from local councils, but this means that over sixty still exist in the British Isles. Some of these are quite large (Leeds owns nearly 700 buses), and others very small (Bedwas & Machen Urban District in South Wales has a fleet of seven). Several of them have arrangements with the local NBC company, so that services are operated jointly, while others prefer to remain quite separate; there is a list at the back of this book.

An exception to all this is the arrangement for providing public services in London, which is the only city in the British Isles to have a substantial underground railway as well (Glasgow has a small one, but in London the underground is much more important). This has made it necessary to treat London separately for a great many years, and since a special Act of Parliament of 1969, we have a London Transport Executive, owned by the Greater London Council. This owns the underground and the red buses. The country buses and Green Line services that were formerly run by London Transport are now the concern of London Country Bus Services Ltd., which was set up by the National Bus Company to run them. The GLC appoints the members of the Executive, which is sometimes like a Passenger Transport Executive, but not quite the same.

Important as these various public bodies are, they by no means provide all the public services that we need, for as we have seen there is a large number of private firms. A few of these are quite substantial, and run regular services over a wide area; others run long distance services linking different parts of the country. But the majority own fewer than twenty-five vehicles, and some 1,800 of them are one-bus concerns. Often these are businesses where the owner is also the driver, and in most cases the proprietor of a small fleet will take a direct part in its management – driving a bus or coach when required, issuing tickets, keeping the books or undertaking the maintenance. The service to the public that these small firms provide is just as important in its way as that of the big companies and the local councils, while in addition they are often able to help the larger firms by providing vehicles for them to hire when they need more than they own themselves.

So far, we have been talking mainly about operators in Great Britain, but to complete the picture let us take a quick look at Ireland. In the Republic it is quite simple: there is one big nationalised company, *Coras Iompair Eireann* (The Irish Transport Company), which owns the railways and the canals as well as most of the buses (there are some thirty-five private bus and coach operators, all quite small, some of whom provide local bus services). CIE runs the Dublin city services, whereas in Northern Ireland the Belfast city services are provided by the city council; the former Ulster Transport Authority which owned all public transport in the province has now been wound up, and the buses are provided by a nationalised company called Ulsterbus Ltd., and by one or two private firms.

The whole of the British Isles is covered by a network of bus services, and as well there is the system of long distance coach services that covers England and Wales and reaches into Scotland. Few European countries have developed such a comprehensive system, largely because most of them imposed restrictions on the growth of bus services in order to make people go on travelling by train. But as well as this network of services, there is a great deal of bus and coach travel that takes place on what are sometimes called 'unscheduled services' – day excursions and special trips of all kinds – and then there are the coaches that run for schools and factories, and are not available to ordinary members of the public. In the next few chapters we shall be looking at the organisation, and at the kinds of service in more detail, but first we shall have a look at the history of this great industry, and see how things have come to be as they are.

CHAPTER 2

How it came about

The ancestry of the bus and coach industry may be traced back to the days of the stage coaches which flourished from the middle of the seventeenth century until they were displaced by the railways in the nineteenth. The service that they provided towards the end of that period was considered at the time to be a great advance on anything that had gone before, and they were widely used, for they provided a network that covered the whole country. In addition, there was a series of special services provided by the Post Office mail coaches, which were faster and more expensive. The railways replaced the coaches wherever they were built, because they could carry more people and so offer lower fares, and because they were so much faster and more comfortable that the public immediately preferred them.

The railway system was constructed very largely between the years 1830 and 1852 (except for the bulk of the lines in Wales and Scotland, which were built during the following twenty years). Thus by the middle of the nineteenth century, people who had any distance to travel used the train for the greater part of their journey. The same period saw the growth of Britain's population at a greater speed than had ever been known, so that the 16 million people of 1830 became 28 million by 1871. And these people were more prosperous too, which meant that they travelled more. Before the railways came, most people stayed in one place all their lives, but when the railways had been built, far more people began to move about. The railways made seaside holidays possible, national newspapers appeared, and many other things that we take for granted today were the result of this great invention.

At first, the railway companies considered their first class passengers more important than anyone else, but after 1872 they began to pay more attention to the others. Bank holidays, which were introduced in 1871, were another opportunity for more people to travel by train, while from the sixties there were more and more 'workmen's' trains, with specially low fares. The idea of going to work by train developed with the growth of cities in the nineteenth century, which in turn had been made possible by the very existence of railways. But the train was by no means the only form of transport for passengers at this time, and horse-drawn transport remained vitally important right into the twentieth century. Unless you lived near to a railway station, you started your journey by some form of road transport (although people were certainly prepared to walk quite long distances in those days). And so, as the old stage coaches disappeared with the growth of the railway system, there appeared a new form of road transport, especially in towns: the omnibus.

The omnibus of the nineteenth century is one of the direct ancestors of the motor bus of the present day. Its special quality, and what made it an immediate success, was a combination of two things: it would stop anywhere on the street to pick up and set down passengers, and it ran regularly to a timetable. The latter was a practice that originated with the stage coaches, but the former had been started by the hackney cabs that first appeared in London about 1625; even so it was uncertain how far it was legal until a special Act of Parliament was passed in 1832. The man who introduced the omnibus to London, on 4 July 1829, was called George Shillibeer, and he copied the idea from what he had seen in France.

Omnibuses became popular in towns and cities all over the country in the years that followed.

The horse-drawn omnibus had its limitations, and the greatest of these was its size. Only two horses were used, because more were awkward to handle in traffic (and traffic congestion in the days of the horse was every bit as serious as it is today). So the size of the bus and the number of people it could carry were limited by the weight that two horses could pull. But the rough roads of the period did not help either, and it was this that gave rise to the invention of the tramcar, which came to be one of the most important means of urban transport.

The first tramcars ran in New York in 1832, and were intended as a means of getting railway carriages right into the centre of the city, by taking them off the train and running them on railway lines laid in the street. The idea caught on, and was introduced to Europe, a line in Paris being opened in 1853. In 1859 an attempt was made to run trams on the dock railway lines of Liverpool, but the man chiefly remembered for introducing tramcars to England, in 1860, was George Francis Train, who was every inch an American. Few of his lines lasted long, however, and in 1862 he went back to the United States.

In 1869 the first real tramway system in Great Britain began to run, in Liverpool, and in 1870 Parliament made it easier for tramways to be built, so that in subsequent years a great many lines were laid. Clearly it was far more expensive to start a tramway service than it was to run an omnibus service, but in spite of that, there were hundreds of places where it was found worthwhile. This was because the tramcar could roll more easily along its rails than the omnibus could run along the rough street, and so the same number of horses could pull a larger vehicle. This in turn meant that more people could be carried, which not only made more profit for the operator, but made it possible for him to charge lower fares, which in turn attracted still more people to use the tramway. Naturally, there had to be enough people around who wanted a service for this to work out, so that tramways were generally built where a lot of people lived in a small area (as in so many Victorian towns and cities). But holiday-makers could sometimes give rise to a big enough demand, as in the case of the line built across the Island of Bute in 1882.

For a time in the later nineteenth century, steam engines were used on tramlines to pull even larger passenger cars, but they made a lot of noise and smoke, and were never really popular. Another system was to have an endless cable running in a slot between the rails, to which the cars were fixed so that they could be pulled along, but this too had its disadvantages (cable cars still run in San Francisco). The successful mechanisation of the tramways came with the application of electric power, and by the end of the century the future of street transport was thought to lie almost certainly with the electric tram. Bristol was the first city to electrify a complete tramway system, which was done between 1895 and 1900.

The electric tramway was yet more expensive to build, but once again it would carry far more people, and as well as that, it could be run quite cheaply from power stations built also to provide lighting. But just as the electric tram was becoming generally adopted for urban transport, the motor bus came along, and eventually replaced it. Electric trams could be quite fast and comfortable, however, and in some parts of the country it became possible to travel quite long distances by them. People were very proud to have an electric tramway in their town, and decorated cars were often run to celebrate local or national events. Even quite small towns built tramway systems, and the motor bus industry came in due course to inherit a great deal of traffic as well as many of its managers from the tramways. One of the benefits of the electric tramways, with their cheap fares, was to make it possible for city people to reach the surrounding countryside more easily. In the country itself, local transport (unless you had a railway station reasonably near) went on depending upon horses well into the twentieth century, and in many places until just after the First World War. For a lot of people this meant travelling by the carrier's cart.

The carriers ran from one or more villages to a local market town, sometimes on market day only, but often on one or two other days as well. A village of any size might have such a service to more than one town, and sometimes there would be more than one carrier. You used the cart to go to market with the produce you had to sell there, and to return with the necessities you had bought, or you could arrange for the carrier to obtain things for you. So the carrier's cart was a form of mixed goods and passenger transport, and as such it was an essential part of life in villages all over the country. You rode rough, with only a plank bench to sit on, and with crates of chickens, baskets of vegetables and rolls of wire netting for company, but it cost very little. When the cart reached the town, it 'put up' in the yard of an inn, and when you had finished your business, you returned to find it waiting to take you home.

The mechanisation of road passenger transport
The motor car, which had been developed in Germany and France,

was almost impossible to use in Britain before 1896 because of the speed limit and the need to have a man walking in front with a red flag. The law was changed in 1896, and in 1898 the first motor buses were being tried out. The first motor bus service was started in Edinburgh on 19 May 1898, and various others followed quickly in different parts of the country.

The new buses were found more successful in quiet towns like Tunbridge Wells than in the big cities (in Birmingham, the Midland Red company actually gave up between 1907 and 1912, and went back to running horse buses). But other successful services were started in remote places, where they could serve as an extension of the railway, or as an alternative to the expensive business of building a new branch line. Some of these were started by private firms, such as the Sutherland Transport & Trading Company in the far north of Scotland, which began running motor buses in place of stage coaches in 1906. Others were started by the railways themselves; both the Great Western and the North Eastern began running buses in 1903, and the Great Western became a bus operator of great importance in later years. In the same year Eastbourne became the first local council to run a motor bus service.

In London a number of firms tried running motor buses, but it was not until 1905 that the new vehicles looked like being successful. The London General Omnibus Company, which had been formed in 1855 in Paris (it was originally a French company), was merged in 1908 with its two most serious competitors, and in the following two years its chief engineer, Frank Searle, designed and produced the X-type and then the B-type double deckers, which were so efficient that the motor bus never looked back. By 1910 there were more motor buses than horse buses in London, and the last London horse bus ran in 1914.

Riding in the early motor buses was very different from what we know today. Apart from the much greater risk of breakdown, the harsh springs and solid rubber tyres made for a rough ride, while the interior was frequently not unlike that of a tram, with wooden seats, sometimes facing each other across a centre aisle. The double deckers had open tops (covered tops were extremely rare before 1920), and the curved staircase from the rear platform seemed very unsafe as you climbed down while the bus was moving. The conductor signalled the driver to stop and start by pulling at a string that ran along the ceiling and rang a bell in the driver's cab. When the conductor was on top, he sometimes had a brass plunger near the stairs, which when he pushed it down pulled the string inside, and so rang the bell. However, the driver's cab was open to the winds, and the conductor could shout down to him just as well.

Open-top double deckers have come back into favour, and certainly it is very pleasant to ride on one when the weather is fine. For wet days the old ones had canvas covers that fitted over the seats, to keep them dry, and you pulled them over your knees to keep *you* dry when you sat down. But by 1939 such buses were already a memory, and the industry had settled down to provide a reliable standard of service that was more comfortable than that offered by the remaining trams. Since the end of the Second World War, the standard of service has been improved still further, while almost all the trams have been withdrawn – the only street tramway remaining is the one along the front at Blackpool.

The railways and the council tramway departments contributed to the growth of the bus industry. Individuals bought buses and put them to work, above all during the years following the First World War, and many of them were successful in founding businesses that could survive. But the large companies of today owe their development, if not always their origin, to certain large-scale interests – holding companies, we would call them now – which grew up to organise and finance the bus and coach industry. Notable among them were the British Electric Traction Company, Thomas Tilling Ltd. and, in Scotland, the Scottish Motor Traction Company. After 1929 the big railway companies took a share in this enterprise, but the foundations had been laid earlier. Since 1948 the member companies in these groups, and others like them, have steadily come into the ownership of the State, and it is these that today form the subsidiaries of the National Bus Company. London had its own group, which was originally based upon the holding company that controlled the tube railways. To begin with, it was American capital that was involved, and the firm of Speyer Brothers of New York played a part in the formation of the group, whose fortunes were for many years in the hands of Albert Stanley (later Lord Ashfield). Stanley himself came from America, and remained in charge of London's transport even when it was transferred to a public corporation in 1933. Because of his policies, the buses, trams and trolleybuses of London were always linked financially with the tube railways, which is an arrangement that still continues.

To find the origins of the long distance coach services, we have to go back once more to the early days of the industry. The early bus operators did not consider lengthy journeys impossible, and the first regular service over a long distance was the daily London–Brighton run that commenced on 30 August 1905. This ran until, almost a year later, an accident on Handcross Hill cast doubts upon the safety of long distance buses, and the development of today's express coach services was delayed. After various holiday services had been started in the years following the First World War, the real start of regular long distance coach operation came on 11 February 1925, on the route between London and Bristol.

The coaches of those days would seem primitive to us, but they were at best as comfortable as the private cars of their day. They were slower than the trains, but they were also a lot cheaper to travel by, and since they often saved you having to change, and meant having a reserved seat, they became very popular; so much so that some were allowed to continue running during the Second World War. Today, they form a very important part of our transport system, but in many ways they are the nearest link we have with the stage coaches of 150 years ago.

CHAPTER 3

Who rides on the buses?

Not so long ago, it was still true to say that most people had ridden by bus or coach so recently as to be able to remember what it was like. Today there is a large number of people who never use public transport, and a generation of children is growing up that will include many who have never ridden on a bus at all. A lot depends upon where you live – if it is in the middle of London, you will probably ride on the buses quite often. If you live in a country village, you will probably go to school on a bus, and very likely go by coach on a school trip to London, or even abroad. If you live in a small town, your school trips may be the only time you go in a bus or a coach.

It is much the same for adults. The bus is still quite essential for most people who live in cities, but elsewhere there are many people who never have occasion to use it. There was a time when this only applied to the wealthy or the privileged (it has been said that Winston Churchill only travelled by bus once in his lifetime), but now it applies to anyone who can drive, and has a car available when it is wanted. In the cities, cars are less useful than they are in other parts of the country, but in the rural areas they are much the most convenient means of transport, and so the use of bus services there is falling off. All the same, a great deal of use is still made of coaches and buses all over the country. People need them for different purposes in various places and at different times of the day or year. As a result, there are certain distinct kinds of use to which buses and coaches can be put, and to some extent there are different kinds of bus and coach for these different uses. In this chapter we will look at the different kinds of service, so as to see who uses each one, and in the next we will look at the different kinds of bus and coach, and the jobs of the people who work in the industry.

We must remember that factors are changing, which is one

reason why the bus and coach industry is quite an exciting place to work in today. But there are certain types of service that do not seem to change a great deal, and to start with let us distinguish between *urban* and *rural* needs, and the services that provide for them.

One reason for making this distinction is the fact that more people own cars in the countryside than in cities and the industrial parts of the country. In the whole of Great Britain, there is a car for at least every five people, which means that statistically above half the families in the country have a car. (It is not quite as much as this, because some cars are owned by companies and a few families have more than one.) In the industrial county of Lanarkshire, in Scotland, there are far fewer cars – about one for every ten people. At the other extreme, the remote and very rural Welsh county of Radnorshire has almost one car for every four people, and most of the unindustrialised counties are similarly placed.

Now the point about all this is the comparison with the areas that have good bus services, and the areas that have not. In Lanarkshire the buses are arranged to run to a regular, frequent timetable on almost every route, and there is a network of routes that brings the buses close to the homes of most of the people. There is not the same need for a car in a place like that as there is in Radnorshire, where there have never been very many bus routes to begin with, and where they never provided a very frequent or regular service. (This in turn followed from the fact that in Lanarkshire there were a lot of people living close together, so that first tram and then bus services could easily be provided. In Radnorshire there were never many people, and they lived in scattered settlements, widely apart, so that there was no chance of providing them with regular and frequent buses – they would have been empty most of the time.) What is true of Lanarkshire is true also of Glamorgan and County Durham; Dorset and Kinross are like Radnorshire in this way. In the rural areas, the private car is coming to be the normal form of transport for the greater part of the population, and since there are many good roads in these areas, this works very well for everyone except the people who don't own a car, or cannot get the use of one when they need it. For them, the bus remains essential, especially since the railway no longer serves the small towns and villages as once it did.

Rural bus services are of two kinds, the inter-urban and the true 'village bus'. Where a village happens to lie on a bus route between two towns, it would get a better service than would otherwise be the case, with perhaps a bus every hour, or even more. In areas where towns are fairly close together, and population is reasonably dense, the network of town-to-town services gives a very useful system of transport for all sorts of journeys, at all times of day. People use such services to get to work or to school; to go shopping and to the cinema; to go to hospitals and clinics; and to visit friends and relations. With a bus passing near your home every hour, seven days a week, you can go when you like and come back when you like. Most bus companies would like to run nothing but this kind of service, which is easy to manage and generally profitable. But however extensive it may be, some people will be left out.

There will always be the villages 'off the beaten track', and if the town-to-town service goes too far out of its way to serve them, it will take so long on its journey that it will cease to attract the people who use it most. And then there are the wide areas of the country where towns are far apart, villages few and far between, and the density of population very low. For such places, the bus can only run infrequently if it is to get enough people to provide even the smallest revenue that can justify a service.

The village bus that runs once a day to take people to work and to school and back, with a few extra trips on market day and Saturday, may well provide an 'adequate' service for those who need it. If the villages are small and the area really remote, a bus once a week for shopping may be 'adequate', and there are some villages in rural areas that have one only once a month. Usually there will be special buses in places like this that take children to school, and these will be arranged by the education authority, but the school may not be in a place that other people want to go to. In the same way, factories sometimes provide special buses from remote areas to take their own workpeople. These school and works buses are just as important to people who live in the country as the regular public services.

The companies owned by the State, through the National Bus Company, provide most of the rural services, including practically all the inter-urban ones, but the small coach proprietors do a useful job in running village buses, which they can generally do more cheaply than the bigger firms. There is a handful of private companies running inter-urban services as well.

Many of the journeys people make on urban buses are made for the same sort of reason that people use the country buses – getting to work and to school, shopping, visiting and the rest. Of course, most of their journeys are likely to be shorter, and so to cost less. And then there is the special use of buses in city centres, where people who live outside use them just for getting about, both for business and pleasure. And these are not only people who live in the suburbs or surrounding country and work in the city, but also the tourists, for whom the top deck offers a special attraction.

While cities and large towns have had buses for many years, and usually had trams before them, more recently there has been a growing need for bus services in small towns where housing estates have grown up on the outskirts. Another type of urban bus service is to be found in the large areas of the country that are neither town nor countryside; the spread of houses and factories that makes up the Black Country is a good example. Services in places like this are almost as frequent as those in more compact cities, and have much the same needs to provide for. They are sometimes even busier, because people may get on and off all the way along the route, while the service running out from a city centre can be running pretty empty towards the outer terminus. The Midland Red bus route between Dudley and Stourbridge is said to be the busiest in the whole of England, for just this reason.

Urban buses are run by a mixture of different types of operators. In London there is London Transport itself, with a handful of small firms helping out in some of the suburbs. In the new Passenger Transport Areas there are the Passenger Transport Executives, and in many other towns and cities there are the bus fleets of the local councils. For historical reasons, some cities (as those in the Potteries) are served by companies, usually but not always belonging to the NBC, and most of the new small-town services are provided by similar companies. Again there is a handful of private firms in this kind of operation, in towns and cities of every size.

This survey pretty well exhausts the work of the bus, and we must now look at the reasons why people travel by coach, and the work the coaches do. But first let us remind ourselves that the distinction is not always very plain, for, especially in country areas, the same vehicle is often used to do more than one type of work. This mostly means that coaches are used to provide village bus services, in between other types of work, but sometimes buses are used for special jobs that are generally the function of the coach, such as moving large numbers of people on a special occasion.

Coach services may be regular, like the *express coach services*, or irregular, like the *excursions*, *tours* and *private hire* that make up a good deal of some operators' work. The earliest vehicles were used for 'outings', and for a while the 'char-a-banc' was a rather looked-down-on kind of coach, so that even today some people do not realise how important the express coach system is as part of the nation's public transport.

Figure 4 shows the basic network of express coach services that covers the whole of England and Wales and penetrates into Scotland. (The long distance inter-urban bus takes its place north of the Border.) In general, the coach services are slower than the railway services, and also cheaper, although the growth of the motorways has made a difference in recent years. But the great value of the express coach for many people is the way it fills the gaps left as the railway services have been concentrated on a limited number of main lines, and some of the cross-country services are of the greatest importance. The express coach services must not be thought of as running principally for seaside holiday-makers, for they carry a far wider range of passengers. But the map shows only the express coach services that run daily all the year round, and the official timetable, in its summer edition, lists a great many more that run only in the holiday season. Others run daily in the summer, and are reduced to three or four days a week in the winter. Naturally, there is more need for the services in the summer, when more people travel, and the really busy days are the Saturdays during July and August when people go to and from holidays, at the seaside and

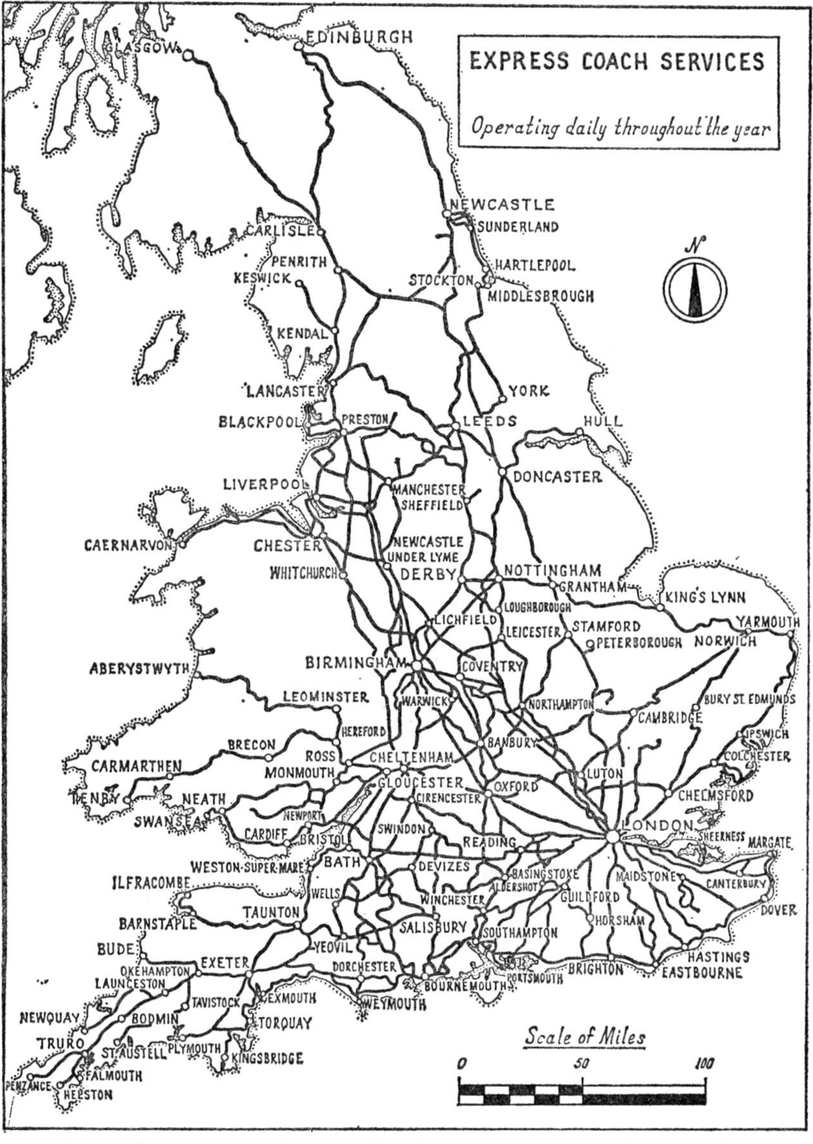

Fig. 4 The express coach network. These are the services that run daily throughout the year; in the summer there are many more

elsewhere. Even the official timetable has not room for all the holiday coach services, some of which may run for no more than five or six days a year, but they are very important for the passengers who use them. Many of these seasonal services provide for special needs, by running direct to a seaside resort that otherwise could only be reached by changing, or by collecting their passengers from the suburbs of a city, and saving them the journey to a central coach or railway station with all their luggage. Others run from smaller towns or even from groups of villages, while yet others go to the smaller seaside resorts, that could not justify a more frequent service.

The regular express coach services, like those shown on the map, are for the most part run by the larger bus companies, which keep special fleets of coaches for the purpose. Not all of them do this, however, while there are one or two sizeable companies whose main business is in this field. The additional services in the summer may be provided by the same type of operator, but a great many of them are run by private firms, some quite small, which have found a local need and are prepared to serve it.

As well as express services, coaches are used for *excursions* and for privately arranged outings which are very similar from the customer's point of view. The social importance of services of this kind is sometimes overlooked, and it should be remembered that a day at the seaside, a trip to London, or a visit to see the illuminations at Blackpool or Southend, can mean a great deal to families living in crowded conditions, or to old people living alone. Shopping trips to buy Christmas presents are more enjoyable when you travel with a party of people you know, and if you live in a small country town, the shops in a city like Leicester or a market such as the one at Romford can often offer lower prices so that you save money even after paying the coach fare. For others, a trip by coach is part of a seaside holiday.

Extended tours have been run (with intervals for two world wars) ever since 1910, and they are another special form of coach operation. They enable people to visit places famous for their scenery and other attractions, at home and on the continent, who find it difficult to plan their own journeys, and prefer to have all the arrangements, including hotel bookings, made for them. In some cases, the coach

1 City transport: buses carrying rush-hour travellers in Coventry

2 A new departure. Only recently have buses been introduced into the centre of Hampstead – and here is the congestion that they have to face

3 The shoppers' bus arriving at Derby

4 The bus at rest: an off-peak scene in Oxford

5 Town-bound bus with experimental fare box to speed up payment

6 Second-hand buses often keep rural routes going. This London Transport bus was bought by new owners, and ran for some years in East Anglia

7 The engineer's department: the bus washing machine in operation

8 The engineer's department: the paint shop

9 The engineer's department: repairs and maintenance

10 A Setright 'Speed' ticket machine, standard for many years on provincial buses

11 An electrically driven ticket machine and automatic change-giver

takes you all the way – this is usual for tours in Great Britain – but for some continental tours the passengers fly to join a coach which is kept across the water for the whole season, or perhaps hired from a continental firm. Such touring demands a great deal of specialised management, and travel agents as well as coach operators arrange continental tours of this kind.

Extended tours are provided by a fairly small range of firms, which include some of the State-owned companies as well as private operators both large and small. Day excursions and private hire, on the other hand, are run at least as much by the small firms as by the large, and some councils, such as Edinburgh and Leeds, provide coaches for tours of the city. One of the reasons why private hire is largely the business of the small firms is the need to have a special licence before you can run any regular service (including an *advertised* excursion); these licences are not easy to obtain, so many small operators are prevented from running such services.

The last type of operation we have to look at is the regular contract, of which the typical example is the school service. In country areas, as we have seen, this is an essential part of the social system, and the school buses have made it possible for pupils to have the benefit of secondary education, wherever they live. They have also enabled education authorities to close many village schools, and so to save a great deal of money (although some people feel that the quality of life in small villages has suffered from this, and it can be quite a hardship for a small child to have to make a bus journey twice a day, perhaps over a fairly long distance). The contract services that take people to work, on the other hand, have allowed many people to go on living in the country, which might not have been possible with the number of farming jobs decreasing so fast.

Work buses and coaches play an important part in industry all over the country, and factories such as those of the British Motor Corporation at Longbridge, near Birmingham, and Cadbury/ Schweppes at Bournville, see fleets of coaches arrive each morning and leave again at the end of the shift. Sometimes such transport is provided by the management, which may even run its own fleet, as in the case of Lesney Toys in London. Usually the factory hires the coaches from an operating firm, but services may be started by

C

operators looking for new ways of making money with their vehicles. Occasionally a man who works in a factory will buy a coach and start a service for himself and his friends. School and works services are almost entirely run by small coach businesses (where they are not in the ownership of the factory or education committee), and some operators keep older buses, bought second-hand from bigger firms or council fleets, to do this kind of work.

The pattern of different kinds of service that has grown up in Great Britain differs from the arrangements in other countries, where circumstances are often difficult to compare. In North America, for example, distances are often so much greater that a 'rural' bus service may have a route length of a hundred miles or more. In United States terms, a bus is a 'transit bus', and an express coach is an 'intercity bus'. Bus operators in the United States are called 'carriers', a word which in Britain applies almost exclusively to the carriage of goods by road. What we would call excursions tend to be labelled 'sightseeing service', while private hire is called 'charter' across the Atlantic. For some reason, the Americans also use the clumsy word 'transportation', and it is a little difficult to distinguish between 'transport', 'transportation' and 'transit' in their use of words. To keep things simple, only the first has been used in this book.

CHAPTER 4

How it is done

Most people can recognise a coach, and tell you why it is not a bus, and the difference between a single decker and a double decker is plain even from the words, without having to see the vehicles at all. But when once you get to know the industry, you soon find that there are more differences than that, and more different types of vehicle. It is true that distinctions are simpler now than they were forty years ago, but different types of vehicles have different purposes, and anyone who wants to know how the industry works must have some understanding of them. (Engineers need to know a great deal more, but while an engineer may be able to manage a bus fleet, you don't *have* to be an engineer to be a good manager.)

The law distinguishes between *stage*, *express* and *contract* 'carriages', and calls all three of them *Public Service Vehicles*. The differences do not mean very much in practice, though it is useful to remember that the official name for any sort of bus or coach is a public service vehicle, often abbreviated to P S V. (There *are* buses, and even coaches, that are not P S Vs: they are the ones used by contractors for carrying their workmen. Since no fares are charged, these buses do not require the special licence needed for a public service vehicle, and so count as rather large private cars.)

We have already seen that in many cases operators use the same bus or coach for different kinds of work. In many more, specialised vehicles are used, because there is so much work of one type for them to do that they need not be used for anything else. Two examples will show what this means, one for bus operation and the other for coach work.

In London and any of the larger cities the need for bus services is such that the vehicles can go up and down all day long, and because they are fully occupied like this, they can be specially designed for the purpose. London Transport has carried standardisation further than any other operator, and the Routemaster double deckers that are used on many of its services were built specially to its own design. Unique in many ways, the Routemaster was intended to suit the special circumstances of bus operation on London's busy streets, and would not suit a hilly inter-urban route in the provinces or Scotland. But then, provincial operators often prefer a bus that can be used on city streets one day and in country lanes the next.

Our second example comes from the United States, where the Greyhound Corporation runs coach services all over the country. Such a large firm can afford to specialise just like London Transport, but it is providing a very different kind of service, and the standard Greyhound coach is designed for very long distance runs. Adjustable aircraft seats, air conditioning, built-in toilets – all these are standard fittings for the long distance Greyhounds, as they are for coaches used on motorway services in Great Britain.

In each of these examples, the vehicles best suited to the needs of the traffic are evolved by the joint efforts of the firms that build them and those that run them in service.

At the opposite extreme from either of these specialised examples lies the standard output of the manufacturers: a range of coaches that can be used for a local service in the country, or a school outing from a town, or a long distance excursion. The small firms depend upon this type of comfortable and economic all-purpose vehicle, quite often bought second-hand. In between there are the various types of bus and coach used by the larger operators, which will be familiar within their areas and yet may seem strange to someone coming from another part of the country.

Buses and coaches are manufactured by a small number of companies, the position being complicated by the fact that no fewer than five different 'makes' – AEC, Bristol, Daimler, Leyland National and Leyland Redline – are all produced by the British Leyland Motor Corporation at its different factories. Bedford and Ford vehicles are made by firms which are owned in the United States, while two of the other makes available in Great Britain are continental – the Metro-Scania, a partnership between an English body-builder and the Swedish firm of Scania-Vabis is one, while the other is the German Mercedes-Benz. This leaves Seddon Motors as the only British manufacturer outside the Leyland Group.

One of the odd things about the manufacturing side of the industry is the way the bus or coach that we see may have been made by two or three different firms, even before we consider the components that will have been bought by the manufacturer from specialist factories. There are three main parts to a heavy vehicle: the *chassis*, or frame, which, with the wheels and axles, is the support for the *body* and *engine*. To save weight, most modern cars are built with a specially strong body, so that a separate chassis is no longer necessary, but while this construction is normal for buses in the United States and on the continent, British buses are usually constructed in the traditional way.

As a result, the bodywork of the vehicles we see will frequently have been constructed by a different firm from the one whose name appears as manufacturer. There are twenty-two body-building firms listed in the trade directory for the industry for 1971, three of which (British Leyland, Mercedes-Benz and Seddon) are also chassis-builders. In addition, most of the chassis manufacturers also build engines, but it is not unknown for one firm to fit engines in buses that have been built by another. One large manufacturer of diesel oil engines, Gardners, does nothing else but sell its products to other manufacturers to fit in their vehicles. Some companies have always been attracted by the idea of building their own vehicles, and a number of improvements have followed from the designs they have produced. The Midland Red company continued to do this until quite recently, and with its special coaches built for service on the M1 between Birmingham and London it introduced the first design specially adapted for motorway operation. But the standard chassis and engine produced by the manufacturers of today is capable of tackling almost every condition likely to be found on our roads, and while we are never likely to see just one type of vehicle, the choice of model that exists today seems quite able to take care of such differences in operation as exist.

This leaves the design of the body and the provision of essential equipment, such as seats and ventilation, to be the main concern of operators when faced with the choice of vehicle. The order of decision will be something like this. In the first place it is necessary to decide whether you need a bus or a coach, and whether there is reason for some special design. Sometimes the answer may be to buy a standard coach body, robust enough to undertake all sorts of work; sometimes a large firm will buy a vehicle that can start its working life as a coach, with luxury seats, and then later can be fitted with bus seats and be used for another ten years on a different kind of service.

One of the things that will influence your choice at this stage is the number of seats likely to be required. Generally you will find that coaches have fewer seats than buses, because the luxury seat takes up more room than the light bus seat, but sometimes there is a special need for extra comfort, and the number of seats may be further cut down to provide more room for the passengers. At the opposite extreme, if your aim is to carry the maximum number of people in the bus, a double decker may be the answer, or you can go beyond the need for seats at all, and decide on something like the London Transport Red Arrow buses, designed to carry a big load of standing passengers over a short distance, with only enough seats for the quieter parts of the day.

The design of the bus or coach will not be entirely in your own hands. Apart from the fact that few operators today can afford to have a body-builder work entirely to his own specification, and then only for a whole batch of vehicles, there are many aspects of design, including all sorts of measurements, which are subject to the control of the Department of the Environment. The Conditions of Fitness and the Construction and Use Regulations specify the maximum permitted length of a bus or coach (12 metres), the maximum permitted width (2.5 metres) and the maximum height (15 feet). The height of entrance steps, the width of gangways, the space to be left between the seats, and the position and size of emergency doors are all laid down by the law in this way. So also are such things as the design and standard of maintenance of the steering gear, the suspension and the brakes, the fuel tank and the lights. Finally, to make sure there is no risk of the bus overturning, it must be possible to tilt the vehicle and bring it back level, to 28 degrees for a double decker and to 35 degrees for a single decker.

One of the things that has to be considered in choosing a vehicle is whether a petrol or a diesel engine should be fitted. If you need a bus that will spend its life working day in and day out on city streets, or if you have in mind a coach suitable for the nightly run between Scotland and London, then there is no question about it; the diesel is the only engine worth while. Indeed it is impossible to buy a double decker with a petrol engine, and the fleets of the large companies are made up entirely of diesel engines.

The diesel engine costs more to buy, but it is more economical in the use of fuel. It is also more robust than the petrol engines, and will generally require less maintenance, although when it does need attention, it tends to need a lot. This means that a diesel-engined vehicle can be kept on the road for longer than a petrol one, but when it comes into the depot for maintenance it will not be available for some time. It is also true that there are more mechanics with experience of petrol engines than know how to service and repair a diesel. Nevertheless, the attraction of the diesel engine is such that the number of petrol-engined buses and coaches is now quite small – only 8,200 in 1968, compared with 71,400 diesels.

This brings us to the need for standardisation, which is one of the main deciding factors in vehicle choice for the large fleet. For every bus or coach on the road, it is necessary to keep a whole range of spare parts so as to be able to repair it in a hurry if need be, or for replacement of worn units when the time comes for an overhaul. Therefore it is less expensive to run only a few standard types, so that the spare parts will go further, and they will also take up less space than they would if you had to keep spares for a wide variety of types. When the industry was growing fast, between 1919 and 1929, there were a great many different makes of vehicle, but this did not matter so much, since there were also a great many operators. Today, when there are a few big operators, there is a bigger reason for standardising on a smaller number of different vehicles – and even the smaller firms find it pays to buy a standard unit, for which spares can easily be obtained.

The people who work on the buses
In the days of the horse buses, the driver's job was considered an especially attractive one. Pay was good, and although the hours were

long, there was security against unemployment, for even in times of hardship, people still had to travel. The conductor was paid less than the driver, but his job was still one worth having. Then there were the regulators, men whose job was to see the buses ran on time; and the clerks who issued the tickets and punch to the conductor, and who checked his money when he paid in. The horses required a small army of men to look after them, for horses were valuable, and big firms like Thomas Tilling's had not only their own stables, but horse infirmaries as well. Many firms built their own vehicles, and all but the smallest would have coach-builders and painters on the staff, as well as harness-makers and men of various other trades associated with the business.

Apart from the disappearance of the horse, things have not changed so very much, save for one big difference. The job of conductor, which remained very much the same on the motor buses and electric trams as it had been in the horse age, seems now to be a disappearing one. This is very largely because men and women today are paid better wages than they used to get for jobs of this kind, and as a result, the bus companies can no longer afford to employ so many of them. Another reason is the greater security that exists in all sorts of other jobs today, which means that one reason for wanting to work on the buses has been taken away. Because bus work still calls for awkward hours and can be quite exhausting too, there are fewer people wanting to take it up, and so the operators find it hard to get enough crews for the buses. Letting the driver collect the fares makes it possible to make do with fewer men and women on the staff.

Fare collection has also been made easier by the development of mechanical devices for the issue of tickets. There are machines suited specially for town or city services, others that are better for inter-urban routes with a longer range of fares, and others again that can be used on the desk at a travel agent's office. Very few bus services today have ticket systems like the old 'Bell Punch', with its rack of tickets of different values in a wide variety of colours. This is partly because such tickets are expensive to buy from the printer and, on top of that, you have to have special precautions to stop them being used improperly. A machine that prints the details on plain paper or card is more expensive to buy, but costs less to operate, and some of the newer ones go a long way towards reducing clerical work, by keeping a record of ticket sales that can be fed straight into a computer when the money has been checked at the end of the day.

The bus driver's work depends very much upon the type of service he is on. The different types of bus and coach are less of a problem, for a trained man can manage any of them without difficulty – indeed, it is becoming more common now for women to drive, as they did in both world wars. In the council fleets and with the bigger companies, a driver is likely to be doing the same sort of work all the time, and since one depot will provide buses for only a few routes, there may not be much variation even in the roads travelled each day. The coaches belonging to the big firms do offer more variation, for the driver may be on an express service one day, and then take an excursion or a private party out the next. It is with the smaller firms, and especially those that have a mixture of services, that the driver can get a wide variety of work, although with them there will rarely be any steady driving up and down city streets.

The city services of the older patterns, with a conductor 'on the back', is giving place to the 'one-man operated' (or OMO) service, where the driver has a ticket machine mounted beside him, or even an automatic system in which the passengers put their money in a slot. Where there is a ticket machine, the driver will have the same responsibility as the conductor would have, for the machine will count the money he takes, as shown by the value of the tickets that it issues. At the end of the day, he will have to pay in the amount shown by the machine, and so he must be careful, not only to get his change right, but also to see that the machine is set to the right fare before he issues a ticket with it. Many drivers welcome the introduction of one-man operation. It means, of course, rather better pay, for the operators usually arrange to share the saving they make by doing without a conductor, and anyway, the driver's responsibility is quite a lot heavier. But just driving a bus on city streets can get tedious, while the OMO duties mean that there are the passengers to talk to. In some country districts, one-man operation has always been the rule, especially where the number of passengers is few, and here the driver can be an important person in the community. He will know every passenger, and carry messages; he will wait for the regular riders; and he will often deliver parcels right to people's doors.

Long distance coach driving requires different skills to city or country bus work. Some men prefer one job, some another. The express coach driver must be prepared to spend a good many nights away from home (the companies usually arrange lodgings), and he is likely to be on his own, with considerable responsibility, for much of his driving time. A leading driver, in charge of a whole convoy of coaches (he is often called the 'service driver') will have to watch the load on each coach, and warn his headquarters if passengers are turning up for whom he may not have room. If relief coaches are starting from points along the route, the relief drivers will have to report to him, and he must see that they are there and have loaded properly. Radio communication has been experimented with, to help the service driver and the controlling staff, but its value is limited by the distance it can cover.

The express coach services are dependent upon a special system for booking seats, since they are not permitted to carry standing passengers, and a good part of their attraction is the fact that you know you won't have to stand. Tickets are supposed to be booked in advance (although if there is room on the coach, the driver will sell you a ticket, or let you buy one at the office). For each journey there will be a *chart*, telling the driver how many people to expect at each point, and how many will get off, and these charts are prepared from the copies of the tickets issued by booking offices and travel agents. One of the most skilled and responsible jobs in the whole industry is the preparation of these charts, and the issue of instructions to offices and agents, telling them how many seats they may book, and when to stop booking, or refer to the chart-room before they sell any more tickets.

Private hire and excursion drivers have a more straightforward job, but they may be more at the beck and call of the passenger. Most coach drivers expect and obtain tips for the extra trouble they take to help their passengers. On extended tours the driver may also be expected to be a courier, explaining what there is to be seen, and taking the responsibility of seeing to it that the passengers are happily settled in at the hotels where they spend the night. On the continental tours, however, it is not unusual for there to be a courier or hostess, whose sole job this is.

Behind the scenes, there are still the vital jobs similar to those of the horse bus days. Ticket clerks issue and check the ticket machines; schedules clerks prepare the duty schedules; booking clerks issue the tickets for express services, excursions, and continental tours, and arrange private hire work. Instead of the horse master and his team of farriers, harness-makers and so on, there is the chief engineer with his staff of mechanics and fitters. Few operators build their own vehicles now, but there are always repair and maintenance jobs to be done, not only to the engine but also to the body, the seats, and to the brakes and lighting. Perhaps the one job that has remained much the same in this department ever since horse bus days is that of the upholsterer, who sees that torn or damaged seats are repaired; but all of them are there for the same real purpose – keeping the buses on the road.

CHAPTER 5

How it is run

Running a small bus or coach company is relatively simple, and provided the owner or manager is prepared to put a good deal of his time into it, the job does not need a great deal of complicated planning. But not all companies stay small, and from the earliest days of the industry, there have been large fleets to manage. For these it is necessary to have a carefully designed structure of management, so that each member of the staff knows where he or she fits in. Senior managers need to know just what their responsibilities are, and who is responsible for other departments of management, with whom they have to co-operate in securing the smooth running of the fleet. And everyone in any business must know who is his superior, and who is responsible to him lower down the scale.

You will see from figure 5 that a bus company is divided into three parts, which we call traffic, engineering, and secretarial. The same practice applies in the case of fleets run by town or city councils, and (subject to more complicated arrangements because of their size) in the London Transport Executive and the Passenger Transport Executives where these have been set up. The diagram is a simple example of the basic structure, and later we will look at a more complicated example from a large provincial company.

At the top of the tree is the Board of Directors, who in a company are elected by the shareholders. In the case of companies owned by the National Bus Company or the Scottish Transport Group, the directors are appointed by the Board of the NBC or the STG, and the *Chairman of the Board* will be one of the senior staff of the 'owning' company or group. Where a fleet is run by a town or city council, the equivalent of the Board will be the Transport Committee, which will be appointed by the council from among its own members, with careful attention to the balance between the different political parties. In these cases the *Chairman of Committee*

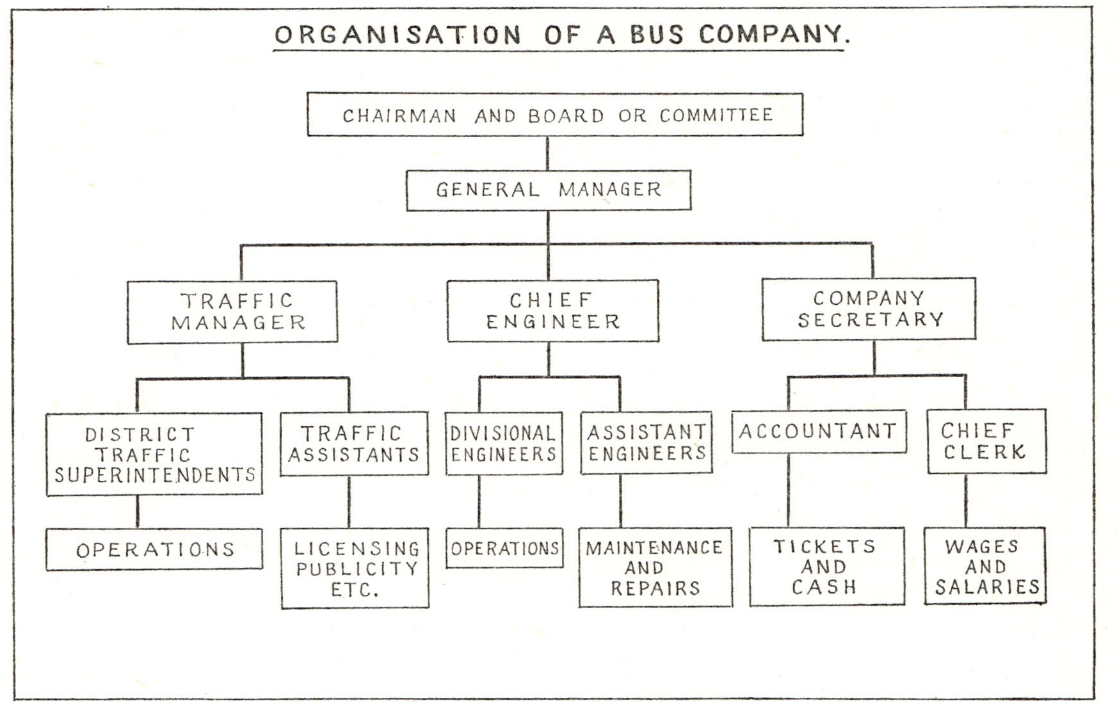

Fig. 5 Simplified chart of the organisation for managing a bus or coach fleet

may be elected from among its members, or again appointment may be made by the council.

The chairman, whether of a large company board or of a municipal transport committee, will not be a full-time officer, although in the case of a company he will probably be paid a fee. It is the *General Manager* who is the full-time officer responsible for the running of the fleet, although it is usual for the chairman and the general manager to meet regularly and keep in close touch over matters of importance. The general manager may be a member of the Board of the company, in which case he is sometimes called the managing director, but he can never be a member of the committee responsible for a municipal fleet. In some medium-sized companies the same man may be both chairman and managing director. Responsible to the general manager are the three chief officers of the organisation. In the diagram, they have been given the titles generally used in the companies, but although they may have different titles in council fleets, their functions are very much the same.

The *Traffic Manager* is responsible for running the buses and coaches on the road. His department arranges the timetables and the schedules of work for drivers and conductors; settles the fares to be charged; obtains the necessary licences for the services run by the undertaking; and plans future development. It is usual for conductors to be the special responsibility of the traffic department, which will arrange their training and the rules governing their work. The traffic department produces a complex series of schedules for the working of the buses and coaches in the fleet, but there will always be more vehicles than the schedules require. Some will be spare, in case of breakdown or sudden extra demand (and there will be spare crews standing by as well). But a certain number will at any time be in the workshops; most of them for regular periodic maintenance, and a few for repair after an accident or breakdown.

The *Chief Engineer* is responsible for the provision of buses and coaches to the traffic department, and for seeing that the fleet is always in good working condition. His department will have a system for the maintenance of the fleet, and when its turn comes, each vehicle must be brought into the workshop, and will not be available for traffic until its maintenance has been seen to. The engineering department may also have a special responsibility for the drivers, and arrange for their training and for the driving test they need in order to be allowed to drive a public service vehicle. There will also be the stores side, and the purchasing of new equipment and spare parts.

The *Company Secretary*, sometimes called the chief accountant, has a special responsibility under company law. He has to keep certain records of the shares issued to those who have invested money in the company, and he will usually be responsible for the company seal. This of course is not an animal, but an embossing stamp, which is used to put the company's official mark on certain special documents, such as share certificates and agreements for purchase of property, or other businesses. The secretary's other main concern is with the financial aspects of running the fleet. He keeps the accounts and prepares the annual statements required by law; he is responsible for the method of fare collection and for seeing that this vital activity is carried out without fault; and he sees to the payment of wages and salaries, as well as preparing the cheques for payment of bills for such things as fuel, spare parts, and for the maintenance and repair of buildings.

Within each of these departments, there will be separate sections responsible for special activities. How many of them there are depends upon the size and nature of the business, but they will generally be of two kinds. The first is based on geography, for where a company has a large area of territory, it will have to set up offices in different places to see to the running of its business locally. At headquarters the three departments will have separate offices, but often in the 'district' or 'divisional' offices, members of the staff of each department will work side by side. The other kind of 'sub-office' will be at the centre, where there may be a separate section dealing with express coach operation, for example, perhaps with an assistant traffic manager in charge. Figures 6 and 7, illustrating the organisation of the Bristol Omnibus Company, show how complex these arrangements may be in a large provincial bus and coach business.

Naturally enough, almost every fleet has a slightly different pattern of management, but the diagrams give a good idea of what

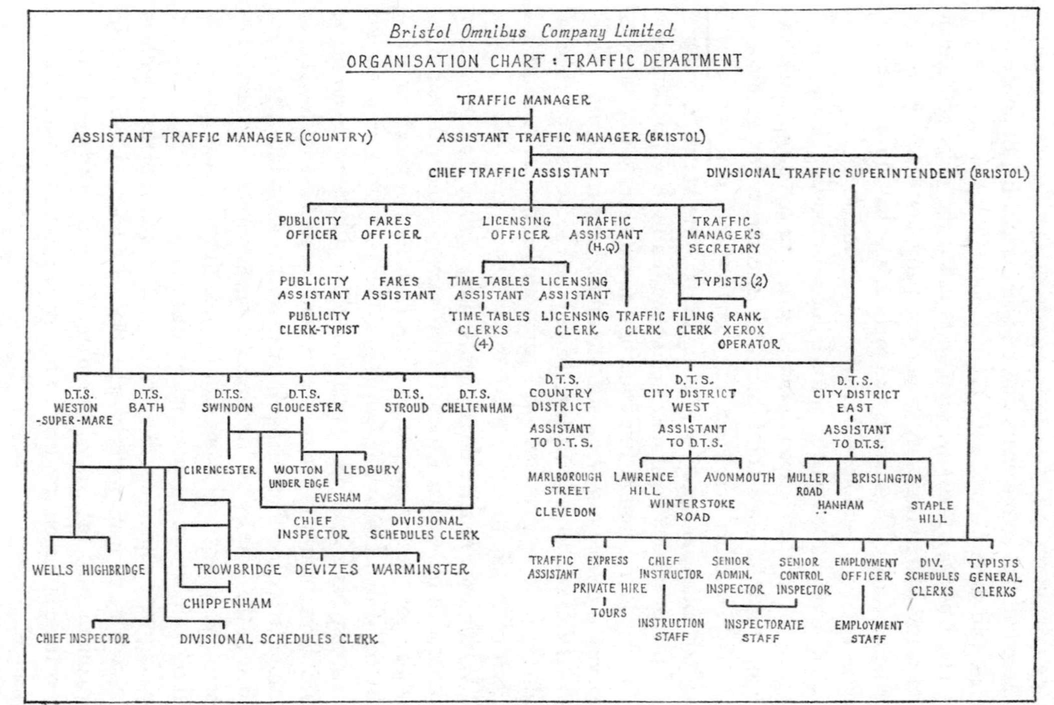

Fig. 6 The traffic organisation of an actual company

12 Where the journey begins. The travel agency is a vital associate of coach operation; this one is actually owned by one of the biggest operators

13 Coach seats have to be booked in advance, whether for services or tours

14 Travel control at Victoria Coach Station. Data from charts is constantly available, so that booking agents may be told what seats are still free at busy times

15 Coach terminal – then. The original departure point for services that today use Victoria Coach Station

16 Coach terminal – now. It was built before the war by London Coastal
Coaches, the company that operates it on behalf of the lines that use it

17 Express coach services play an important part in many people's lives.
These passengers are boarding at Victoria Coach Station

18 This 60-seater double decker coach can run between Preston and London in 4½ hours, including a break of 30 minutes for refreshments

19 Private hire work is a substantial part of coach operation. Here, passengers are joining a hired vehicle

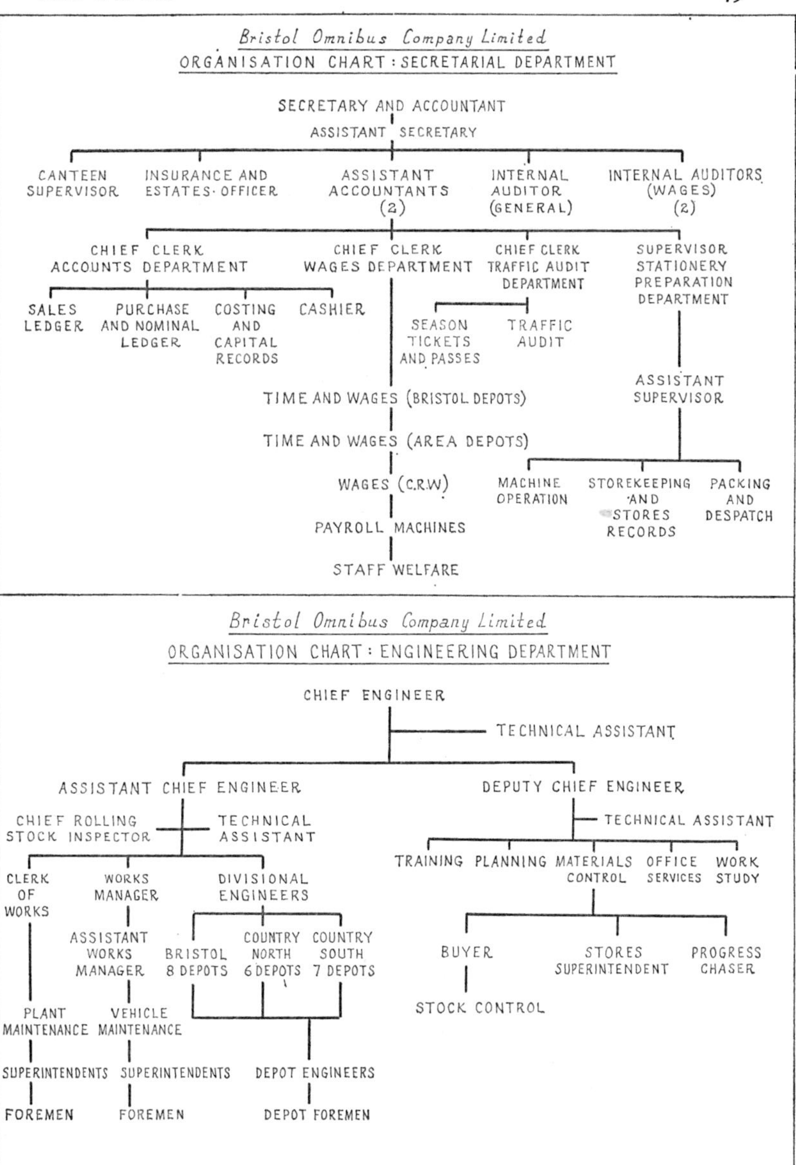

Fig. 7 The secretarial and engineering organisation of an actual company

D

is typical. The main differences will be found in the smaller businesses, which are simply not big enough for such a complex
organisation. Here it is not uncommon to find the proprietor acting
as general manager, with one assistant, often called 'the manager',
who is both traffic manager and secretary/accountant. The engineering side will be the responsibility of a foreman, who may be called
'the engineer', but quite often the proprietor will take charge of this
side of things himself. It is possible for a business to own twenty
or thirty vehicles, and still to manage very well with such an
organisation as this, although in such cases the annual accounts will
be prepared by a firm of professional accountants, and the major
maintenance and repair work may be undertaken by a commercial
garage.

The State and the buses

Most people accept that the provision of a public service cannot be
left to the managers to get on with without some form of supervision by the State. Private firms may be tempted to save money
by reducing the amount spent on maintenance (even city councils
have been known to let this side of management suffer), while it
is not always easy for managers to control the way their vehicles are
being driven, and a bus or coach driver has great responsibilities.
For over a hundred years the State has taken great pains to make the
railways safe, and there are special government officials who are
responsible for safety in factories and for the control of food and
drugs to protect our health. In the case of a bus fleet, the controlling
authority set up in 1919 was the Ministry of Transport, which is
now a part of the Department of the Environment. Before 1930
there was very little control over the operation of buses and coaches,
and what there was depended upon the local councils, which varied
a lot in the extent to which they took their responsibilities seriously.
As a result of an Act of Parliament of that year, a system of control
was set up which has not been changed very much ever since, and
which works by requiring several different licences to be held by
any person, company or council that owns a fleet of public service
vehicles.

The first licence needed is called a *Public Service Vehicle Licence*, and there has to be one for every bus or coach in the fleet before it can be used (it can be driven about empty with only the licence you have to have for a private car). But this licence is not enough by itself, for along with it goes a *Certificate of Fitness*. The P S V Licence will be taken away if the operator misbehaves seriously in the way he runs his business – for example, if he persistently fails to maintain his vehicles properly, or if he is always letting them run late without good reason. The Certificate of Fitness has to be re-newed every so often, and eventually it will be refused, because the vehicle has become too old and decrepit to be safe. The officials of the Ministry can examine a vehicle at any time, and take away its certificate if they think fit, until such time as it has been put in order again.

These two licences see to it that the vehicles are safe, and that the fleet is properly managed. The next two concern the men and women who work on the buses. You have to have an ordinary driving licence before you can drive a bus or coach, but you also have to have a special additional one, called a *PSV Driver's Licence*. To get it, you have to be at least twenty-one and you will need a medical certificate (with a special eyesight test) and a certifi-cate of good character. You will then have to pass an additional, very stiff driving test, with a bus of the size you want to drive.

A conductor requires a *PSV Conductor's Licence*, and must be at least eighteen. A certificate of good character is required, but there is no equivalent to the driving tests.

With these licences, you can put a bus or coach on the road to earn money for you by carrying passengers, but there are a number of things you must not do with it unless you have the authority of yet another document, the *Road Service Licence*. You need this before you can run any regular service, advertised to the public in advance (including excursions and tours). You even need it to run continental tours, if you are going to carry passengers by coach to the sea or air ferry terminal in this country, which is why many tours are arranged so as to fly parties across the Channel to join a coach kept overseas. As we have seen, without a Road Service Licence, you can only use your vehicle for private parties, or for a school bus service, or for taking people to work at a factory and paid for by the factory managers.

The way the law stands, it is not easy to get a Road Service Licence, and firms who already hold a number of them, like the big companies in the NBC group or in Scotland, have a better chance of getting new ones than do newcomers. This means that such a licence is a valuable possession, for it makes it almost impossible for any new firm to start up in competition with the holder of one. In return for this privilege, the State lays down in the licence the time and fare tables that are to apply to the service, and often the number of vehicles that may be used on it.

The operator starts by saying what he wants these to be, but once they are stated on the licence, he has to keep to them, unless he is given special permission to change them. You cannot do this very quickly, and the result is that fares cannot easily be altered. Consequently management cannot be constantly changing prices to meet changes in the cost of operation and in the needs and demands of the public. Some would therefore argue that the law is too strict in this way.

The Minister of Transport appoints a number of people to run the system of control by licences. The country is divided up into eleven traffic areas, and for each there is a licensing authority, called the *Traffic Commissioners*. The Commissioners are responsible for all the licences except the Certificate of Fitness, which is issued by the *Certifying Officer* for the area. Where there is a dispute, appeals are decided by the Minister. The managers of a bus or coach fleet will have a great deal to do with these people and their staff, the chief engineer dealing mainly with the certifying officer, and the traffic manager with the Traffic Commissioners. When a new service is being planned, the application for a Road Service Licence is publicly announced, and all sorts of people may object. When they do, the Traffic Commissioners will hold an enquiry, and the applicant and objectors will appear, and members of the public will be asked to go along and say that they want the new service. These enquiries, which are nothing like as formal as a court of law, are commonly called Traffic Courts.

It is important to remember that the whole of the industry, with only small exceptions, comes under this system of control. The big companies that are owned by the State, through the National Bus Company and the Scottish Bus Group, still have to have the same licences. The only exceptions are the special position of London Transport, mainly in being free from road service licensing in central London, and the freedom for operators to use very small buses without such licences. As things stand, the Passenger Transport Executives are also to be in a special position in due course, but it may be that the law will be changed on this point.

The government is planning to make a number of changes in the law relating to road service licences, but final details were not available when this book went to press. They were expected to make it easier for operators to increase their fares, and to alter the licence requirements for certain types of service.

CHAPTER 6

A career with the buses

The bus and coach industry today is faced with bigger problems and a greater likelihood of change than ever before in its history. In this book we have examined the way the industry is run now, but for those of the new generation who choose to make it their career, what we have seen may come to look out of date before very long.

The great hope of the industry lies in the willingness of those who enjoy running buses and coaches to seek for new answers to new problems, and to find new techniques to use as old ones cease to be any use. The problems of the industry are different in the different kinds of operation that we have described. In towns there is the difficulty of running a reliable service through congested streets, which makes people prefer to use a car if they can – and that makes congestion worse again! It is not easy to tempt enough people back on to the buses to make a serious difference to the number of cars on the road, and the alternative, of banning cars from city centres, is not as easy as it sounds. Some people go so far as to advocate charging no fares at all for urban services, but this could easily make things worse. Probably the most promising approach is for management to pay much closer attention to the sort of things people want, and to try to adjust the service to them – the service required isn't always obvious, and it may be different in different places.

In the country the problem is different again, for there is no congestion, but the private car offers people a much better service than the bus possibly can, which is why more people own cars in the country districts than in the towns. In many places this means that there are not enough passengers left to make the country services pay, yet the remaining people need the bus just as much as ever they did. One answer may be to take money from local taxation to pay for services that do not earn enough to keep going; another may be to encourage the smaller operators to take them over where the bigger ones cannot keep going, for the smaller firms usually have lower costs.

Long distance coach services are one part of the industry that seems still to be doing well, and coaches are going to be wanted for private parties, and for school and workmen's services, as far ahead as we can foresee. Extended tours, at home and abroad, are still very popular with holiday-makers, although day excursions often suffer from the congestion that surrounds some of our holiday resorts.

New techniques that are already being tried include door-to-door services for people going to and from work. An experiment of this kind is being carried out at Stevenage, where London Country Bus Services are running special Blue Arrow buses, and another at Leeds, where the City Transport Department has a number of new ideas. At Manchester the Passenger Transport Executive has started a special Executive Express which is a luxury coach, complete with hostess and refreshments, to tempt people out of their cars in the rush hour. Another idea that has been tried out in London and a number of other places is the use of special 'bus lanes', allowing the buses to move freely, and even to go against the ordinary flow of traffic. The city of Leicester has a most comprehensive plan to allow the use of the private car to continue alongside the sensible use of public transport.

Inter-urban transport has not been neglected either, in the development of new ideas. With the railways concentrating on the longer distances, there is a need for good public transport between

Service	Time taken by:		
	Old-style bus	Train	White Rose
Sheffield/Leeds	145 mins.	65 mins.	55 mins.
Sheffield/Bradford	170 mins.	100 mins.	95 mins.
Sheffield/Halifax	130 mins.	115 mins.	85 mins.
Rotherham/Leeds	135 mins.	55 mins.	45 mins.
Mexborough/Leeds	125 mins.	75 mins.	70 mins.
Sheffield/Barnsley	55 mins.	35 mins.	25 mins.

Source: Diagram in NBC *Review of 1969*, p. 20 (figures rounded).

cities that are fairly close together, and the motorways offer a chance to make this possible. White Rose Expressway is a group of four NBC companies and three council fleets, which runs a highly successful network of services in the West Riding of Yorkshire, all developed since October 1969. The table on page 55 shows the advantage the White Rose services have over both train and old-style bus.

It seems likely that new ways of using existing forms of transport, such as the bus, are going to be more valuable than entirely new techniques, such as the monorail. If you are going to build an entirely new city, you can afford to design it round a new form of transport, while on the other hand, it is almost impossibly expensive to convert an existing city overnight to a new technique, and even more so to do it a piece at a time. The advantage of the bus is its flexibility, and the fact that it is cheap to operate as well as being cheap to buy, so that it looks as if it will go on being used for a long time yet. Even if we have to abandon the diesel or petrol engine because of what it may be doing to the atmosphere, a public service with some other sort of engine – electric, or even steam, or the fuel cell, for example – will still be a bus, and the job of running a fleet of these new-type buses will not be greatly changed.

If you are interested in this job of running buses, which is a demanding one, and which needs a good deal of education and ex-perience if it is to be done well, there are a number of ways of making it your career. If you are mechanically minded, you can qualify as a mechanical engineer, and specialise in this side of the business. To reach a position of responsibility on the engineering side, you need to have some training in the art of management, for you will have to run a large department in any of the bigger firms. Organising the running and maintenance of a fleet of buses or coaches takes its own skill, and doing so economically is going to be more important than ever in the future. In a small firm, or in many council transport departments, the chief engineer may well be the manager, so that there is room for people who can combine the skills of engineering with the ability to look after the traffic side.

If you are good with figures, there is a career to be made on the accounting and secretarial side, and with the great importance of the computer in modern industry, this is likely to become a more extensive responsibility than that held by chief accountants in the past. The use of a computer to record the statistics of a bus fleet – the numbers of passengers carried, the revenue, and even the financial surplus of each service – offers new methods of providing information for management. In the past, such figures have been rudimentary, and often have taken a long time to produce, because all the work had to be done by hand. But the computer can not only make the calculations with enormous speed and accuracy; it can carry a very great deal of information in its memory bank, and can combine this information in many different ways. The bus industry has hardly begun to work out the ways in which this kind of ability can be put to use, but there is a great future for anyone who can combine the computer skills with the understanding of the way bus fleets are run.

For anyone who is interested just in 'running buses', though, the best career is still with the traffic department. Many people in the past have risen to the top in this way, with little formal training for the job, which has seemed to require more instinct than education. Today we are realising the hard fact that the economics of a bus fleet is by no means as straightforward as might appear, while the new techniques of management (such as market research for example) require a good grasp of mathematics. In the days when you could put on a bus service, and sit back and wait for people to come and ride in your buses (and this was still broadly true twenty years ago), life was easy for the traffic side. Now that you have got to fight the competition of the private car, and tempt people away from the television set, the traffic manager has to *sell* his services. He has to find out carefully what the potential customer wants, and provide as close a service as he can to meet this demand, at the same time keeping his costs down so that people can afford to pay the fares he has to ask.

One side of management, in all departments, is the need to be able to deal fairly and properly with the people working for you, and with their representatives, the shop stewards and trade union officers. The engineering and accountancy departments have this

E

responsibility as much as the traffic side, but for the traffic manager the problem is greater because here the duty schedules of the drivers and conductors have to be prepared and agreed. These schedules must not only make economic use of manpower, by ensuring that the buses are moving as much of the time as possible (a stationary bus will earn nothing), but they must also be fair to the staff, and on top of everything else they must comply with the law that governs the number of hours a driver may work. Yet just to fulfil all these conditions is not enough, for the 'road staff' are the people in contact with the public. They have a highly skilled job to perform, and it is only when they feel themselves to be part of a good team, whose objectives and rewards they share, that they will take the extra care necessary for the satisfaction of the customer.

Fortunately, there are a number of schemes of management training in the bus and coach industry. If you join one of the larger companies, or a municipal transport department, you can expect to be given an introductory training course, and in many cases to have regular time off during the day to study for the examination of the Institute of Transport at your local technical college. If you start with a smaller firm, you are likely to be nearer to the senior managers, and while you may not be given systematic training, you will be able to learn a good deal by keeping your eyes open, and by asking questions when there is an opportunity to do so. For the top posts in the industry there is also the special training offered by the National Bus Company, which selects management trainees for a two-year course in all branches of bus and coach management.

The NBC training scheme is open to people coming straight from school, or from university, but equally available to people who have already started work in the industry. The two years are spent with one of the NBC's operating companies (see figure 2) under the supervision of its general manager. Towards the end of the period, the trainee will be working in the general manager's office, but before that he will have obtained direct experience of all departments of management. If he has not taken the Institute of Transport examinations, he will be required to do so, and given time for the purpose. He will be paid a salary while in training, and at the end of the two years he can expect an appointment, if he has completed the training satisfactorily, that will be at a level of responsibility either in the company that has trained him or in another. While the scheme does not prevent people from rising to the top without passing through such a course, there is no doubt that it offers a most valuable and attractive introduction to a career in the bus and coach industry.

Some of the largest fleets will require their own doctor or architect, and there may be special posts such as that of personnel manager, training officer or public relations officer. In all of them, an understanding of what running buses and coaches is about goes alongside the other special qualifications required.

The most important thing that the bus and coach industry looks for in those who are thinking about making it their career is the sort of enthusiasm that makes people willing to work hard, combined with the ability to look at things as they are. More and more young people are looking to transport in general for an interesting and rewarding career, and bus and coach operation, with all the problems that it has to face in the coming years, is one of the most fascinating branches of transport. It has room for women in it as well as men (although this possibility is only now being recognised). If you want the sort of job that is really important for helping people, and one that is always offering new interest and new challenge, then running a bus or coach fleet may well be the place for you.

Bus and coach operators in the British Isles

A – Nationalised Companies

ENGLAND AND WALES

Birmingham & Midland Motor Omnibus Co. Ltd. (*Midland Red*),
Midland House, 1 Vernon Road, Edgbaston, Birmingham 16.

Black & White Motorways Ltd., Coach Station, St Margaret's Road,
Cheltenham, Glos.

Brighton, Hove & District Omnibus Co. Ltd., Conway Street,
Hove BN3 3LT.

Bristol Omnibus Co. Ltd., Berkeley House, Lawrence Hill,
Bristol BS5 0DZ.

Cheltenham District Traction Company, Berkeley House, Lawrence Hill,
Bristol BS5 0DZ.

Crosville Motor Services Ltd., Crane Wharf, Chester CH1 3SQ.

Cumberland Motor Services Ltd., PO Box 17, Tangier Street, Whitehaven,
Cumberland.

Eastern Counties Omnibus Co. Ltd., PO Box 10, 79 Thorpe Road,
Norwich NOR 81A.

Eastern National Omnibus Co. Ltd., 48–49 New Writtle Street, Chelmsford,
Essex.

East Kent Road Car Co. Ltd., Station Road West, Canterbury, Kent.

East Midland Motor Services Ltd., New Street, Park Road, Chesterfield,
Derby.

East Yorkshire Motor Services Ltd., 252 Anlaby Road, Hull HU3 2RS.

Gosport & Fareham Omnibus Company (*Provincial*), Hoeford, Fareham,
Hants.

Greenslades Tours Ltd., 29 Paris Street, Exeter, Devon.

Hants & Dorset Motor Services Ltd., The Square, Bournemouth BH2 5AB.

Hebble Motor Services Ltd., Walnut Street, Halifax, Yorks.

Jones' Omnibus Services Ltd., Aberbeeg Road, Aberbeeg, Mon.

Keighley-West Yorkshire Services Ltd., PO Box 24, East Parade, Harrogate,
Yorks.

Lincolnshire Road Car Co. Ltd., Omnibus Station, St Marks, Lincoln.

London Country Bus Services Ltd., Bell Street, Reigate, Surrey.

Maidstone & District Motor Services Ltd., Knightrider House,
    Knightrider Street, Maidstone, Kent.

Mansfield District Traction Company, Mansfield Road, Heanor DE7 7BG.

Midland General Omnibus Co. Ltd., Mansfield Road, Heanor DE7 7BG.

Northern General Transport Co. Ltd., 117 Queen Street, Gateshead
    NE8 2UA.

North Western Road Car Co. Ltd., Charles Street, Stockport SK1 3JU.

Nottinghamshire & Derbyshire Traction Company, Mansfield Road,
    Heanor DE7 7BG.

Oxford, City of, Motor Services Ltd., 395 Cowley Road, Oxford.

Potteries Motor Traction Co. Ltd., Woodhouse Street, Stoke-on-Trent
    ST4 1EQ.

Red & White Services Ltd., Bulwark, Chepstow, Mon.

Ribble Motor Services Ltd., Frenchwood Avenue, Preston, Lancs.
    PR1 4LU.

Samuelson New Transport Co. Ltd., 3 Eccleston Place, London S.W.1.

Shamrock & Rambler Coaches Ltd., 77 Holdenhurst Road, Bournemouth,
    Hants.

Sheffield United Tours Ltd., Charlotte Road, Sheffield 2.

Southdown Motor Services Ltd., PO Box 6, Southdown House,
    Freshfield Road, Brighton BN2 2BW.

Southern Vectis Omnibus Co. Ltd., Nelson Road, Newport, I.O.W.

South Wales Transport Co. Ltd., 31 Russell Street, Swansea, Glam.

Standerwick, W. C., Ltd., Rigby Road, Blackpool, Lancs.

Sunderland District Omnibus Co. Ltd., 117 Queen Street, Gateshead
    NE8 2UA.

Thames Valley and Aldershot Omnibus Co. Ltd. (*Alder Valley*),
    Thorn Walk, Reading, Berks.

Tillings Travel (NBC) Ltd., 48–49 New Writtle Street, Chelmsford, Essex.

Timpson, A., & Sons Ltd., 175 Rushey Green, Catford, London S.E.6.

Trent Motor Traction Co. Ltd., Uttoxeter New Road, Derby DE3 3NJ.

Tynemouth & District Transport Co. Ltd., 117 Queen Street, Gateshead
    NE8 2UA.

Tyneside Omnibus Co. Ltd., 117 Queen Street, Gateshead NE8 2UA.

United Automobile Services Ltd., United House, Grange Road, Darlington,
    Co. Durham.

United Counties Omnibus Co. Ltd., Bedford Road, Northampton
    NN1 5NN.

Venture Transport Co. (Newcastle) Ltd., 37 Medomsley Road, Consett,
  Co. Durham.

Western National Omnibus Co. Ltd., National House, Queen Street,
  Exeter EX4 3TF.

Western Welsh Omnibus Co. Ltd., 253 Cowbridge Road West, Ely,
  Cardiff.

West Riding Automobile Co. Ltd., Belle Isle, Wakefield, Yorks.

West Yorkshire Road Car Co. Ltd., PO Box 24, East Parade, Harrogate,
  Yorks.

Wilts & Dorset Motor Services Ltd., 8–10 Endless Street, Salisbury, Wilts.

Yorkshire Traction Co. Ltd., Upper Sheffield Road, Barnsley, Yorks.

Yorkshire Woollen District Transport Co. Ltd., Savile Town, Dewsbury,
  Yorks.

York–West Yorkshire Joint Committee, PO Box 24, East Parade,
  Harrogate, Yorks.

SCOTLAND

Alexander, W., & Sons (Fife) Ltd., Esplanade, Kirkcaldy, Fife.

Alexander, W., & Sons (Midland) Ltd., Brown Street, Camelon, Falkirk.

Alexander, W., & Sons (Northern) Ltd., Bus Station, Guild Street,
  Aberdeen AB9 2DR.

Central SMT Co. Ltd., Traction House, Motherwell, Lanarks.

Highland Omnibuses Ltd., Farraline Park, Inverness.

Scottish Omnibuses Ltd., New Street, Edinburgh 8.

Western SMT Co. Ltd., Nursery Avenue, Kilmarnock, Ayrshire.

IRELAND

Coras Iompair Eireann, Heuston Station, Dublin 8.

County Donegal Railways Joint Committee, Stranorlar, Lifford,
  Co. Donegal.

Ulsterbus Ltd., Milewater Road, Belfast BT3 9BG.

B – *Passenger Transport Executives, etc.*

London Transport Executive, 55 Broadway, Westminster, London S.W.1.

Merseyside Passenger Transport Executive, 24 Hatton Garden, Liverpool
  L3 2AN.

South East Lancashire & North East Cheshire Passenger Transport
  Executive (SELNEC), Peter House, Oxford Street, Manchester M1 5AW.

Tyneside Passenger Transport Executive, Erick House, Princess Square, Newcastle upon Tyne NE1 8EY.

West Midlands Passenger Transport Executive, Pitmaston, Moor Green Lane, Moseley, Birmingham 13.

C – Municipal Transport Departments

ENGLAND AND WALES

Aberdare UDC Transport Dept., Gadlys, Aberdare, Glam.

Accrington Corporation Transport Dept., 142 Blackburn Road, Accrington, Lancs.

Barrow-in-Furness Corporation Transport, Hindpool Road, Barrow-in-Furness, Lancs.

Bedwas & Machen UDC Omnibus Dept., Newport Road, Bedwas, Mon.

Blackburn Corporation Transport Dept., 15–17 Railway Road, Blackburn BB1 5AZ.

Blackpool Corporation Transport, Blundell Street, Blackpool FY1 5DD.

Bournemouth Corporation Transport, Mallard Road, Bournemouth BH8 9PN.

Bradford City Transport, Forster Square, Bradford 1.

Brighton Corporation Transport, Lewes Road, Brighton, Sussex.

Burnley, Colne & Nelson Joint Committee, Queensgate, Colne Road, Burnley, Lancs.

Burton upon Trent Corporation Transport Dept., Guild Street, Burton upon Trent, Staffs.

Caerphilly UDC Transport Dept., Omnibus Garage, Mill Road, Caerphilly, Glam. CF8 3FF.

Calderdale Joint Omnibus Committee, Halifax, Yorks.

Cardiff, City of, Transport, Wood Street, Cardiff.

Chester Corporation Transport Dept., Station Road, Chester.

Chesterfield Corporation Transport Dept., Stonegravels Depot, Sheffield Road, Chesterfield, Derby.

Colchester Corporation Transport Dept., Magdalen Street, Colchester, Essex.

Colwyn Bay Borough Council Transport, Civic Centre, Colwyn Bay, Denbigh.

Coventry Corporation Transport, 113–117 Harnall Lane East, Coventry, Warks.

Darlington (County Borough) Transport Dept., 10 Houndgate, Darlington,
  Co. Durham.
Darwen Corporation Transport, Blackburn Road, Darwen, Lancs.
Derby Corporation Omnibus Dept., Ascot Drive, Derby DE2 8ND.
Doncaster Corporation Transport Dept., Leicester Avenue, Doncaster,
  Yorks.
Eastbourne Corporation Transport Dept., Churchdale Road, Eastbourne,
  Sussex.
Gelligaer UDC Omnibus Dept., New Road, Tiryberth, Hengoed
  CF8 7XG.
Great Yarmouth Corporation Transport, Caister Road, Great Yarmouth,
  Norfolk.
Grimsby & Cleethorpes Transport Joint Committee, Victoria Street,
  Grimsby, Lincs.
Hartlepool Corporation Transport, 67 Church Street, Hartlepool, Co.
  Durham.
Huddersfield Corporation Transport Dept., 66 John William Street,
  Huddersfield, Yorks.
Ipswich Corporation Transport Dept., Constantine Road, Ipswich, Suffolk.
Kingston upon Hull Corporation Transport, Lombard Street,
  Kingston upon Hull, Yorks.
Lancaster City Transport, Kingsway, Lancaster.
Leeds City Transport, 1 Swinegate, Leeds LS1 4DQ.
Leicester City Transport, Abbey Park Road, Leicester.
Lincoln City Transport Dept., St Mark's, Lincoln.
Llandudno UDC Transport Dept., Builder Street West, Llandudno,
  Caernarvonshire.
Lowestoft Corporation Transport Dept., Rotterdam Road, Lowestoft,
  Suffolk.
Lytham St Annes Corporation Transport Dept., Squires Gate,
  Lytham St Annes, Lancs.
Maidstone Corporation Transport Dept., Armstrong Road, Maidstone,
  Kent.
Merthyr Tydfil Corporation Passenger Transport Dept.,
  Nantygwenith Street, Merthyr Tydfil, Glam.
Morecambe & Heysham Corporation Transport Dept., Heysham Road,
  Morcambe & Heysham, Lancs.
Newport Corporation Transport, 160 Corporation Road, Newport,
  Mon. NPT 0WF.

Northampton Corporation Transport, St James', Northampton.

Nottingham City Transport, Lower Parliament Street, Nottingham
NG1 1GG.

Plymouth, City of, Transport, Milehouse, Plymouth, Devon.

Pontypridd UDC Transport Dept., Treforest, Pontypridd, Glam.

Portsmouth, City of, Passenger Transport Dept., Highland Road, Southsea,
Portsmouth PO4 9HE.

Preston Corporation Passenger Transport Dept., Central Bus Station,
Preston PR1 1YX.

Reading Corporation Transport, Mill Lane, Reading, Berks.

Rossendale Joint Transport Committee, Bacup Road, Rawtenstall, Lancs.

Rotherham Corporation Transport, Transport Building, Frederick Street,
Rotherham, Yorks.

St Helens Corporation Transport, Shaw Street, St Helens, Lancs.

Sheffield Transport Dept., Exchange Street, Sheffield S5 2SZ.

Southampton, City of, Transport Dept., 226 Portswood Road,
Southampton.

Southend-on-Sea Corporation Transport, Civic Centre, Southend-on-Sea,
Essex SS2 6ER.

Southport Corporation Transport Dept., Municipal Buildings,
1 Eastbank Street, Southport, Lancs.

Sunderland Corporation Transport Dept., Monkwearmouth, Sunderland,
Co. Durham.

Swindon Corporation Passenger Transport Dept., Transport Offices,
Corporation Street, Swindon, Wilts.

Teesside Municipal Transport, Parliament Road, Middlesbrough, Teesside
TS1 5PG.

Warrington Corporation Transport Dept., Wilderspool Causeway,
Warrington, Lancs.

West Monmouthshire Omnibus Board, Blackwood, Mon.

Widnes Corporation Motor Omnibus Dept., Moor Lane, Widnes, Lancs.

Wigan Corporation Transport Dept., Market Place, Wigan, Lancs.

SCOTLAND, IRELAND AND ISLE OF MAN

Aberdeen Corporation Transport Dept., 2 Marischal Street, Aberdeen.

Belfast Corporation Transport Dept., Utility Street, Belfast BT12 5JT.

Douglas Corporation Transport Dept., Stratallan Crescent, Douglas, I.O.M.

Dundee Corporation Transport Dept., Friarfield House, Barrack Street,
Dundee.

Edinburgh Corporation Transport, 14 Queen Street, Edinburgh EH2 1JL.

Glasgow Corporation Transport, 46 Bath Street, Glasgow C2.

D – Independent Bus and Coach Firms owning 50 vehicles or more

GREAT BRITAIN

Alexander, T. D., & Sons Ltd., Surbiton Street, Sheffield 9 (and at Arbroath, Angus).

Ayrshire Bus Owners (A1 Service) Ltd., Parkhouse Road, Ardrossan, Ayrshire.

Banfield, Chas. W., Ltd., 20–26 Nunhead Lane, London S.E.15.

Barr & Wallace Arnold Trust Ltd., 21 The Calls, Leeds 2 (and at Scarborough, Torquay, etc.)

Barton Transport Ltd., High Road, Chilwell, Notts.

Bee Line Roadways Ltd., 436 Linthorpe Road, Middlesbrough, Teesside.

Bere Regis & District Motor Services, 7 Bridport Road, Dorchester, Dorset.

Blackbourn, A. & A. E., Ltd., Norfolk House, Welholme Road, Grimsby, Lincs. (and at Great Yarmouth, etc.).

Don Everall Travel Ltd., Bilston Road, Wolverhampton, Staffs.

Grey Green Coaches Ltd., 53–55 Stamford Hill, London N.16.

Hall's Coaches Ltd., Clipstone House, Hospital Road, Hounslow, Middx.

Harper Bros. (Heath Hayes) Ltd., Heath Hayes, Cannock, Staffs.

Lancashire United Transport Ltd., Atherton, Lancs.

Lloyd, J., & Sons Ltd., Avenue Road, Nuneaton, Warks.

Mulleys Motorways Ltd., High Street, Ixworth, Bury St Edmunds, Suffolk.

Premier Travel Ltd., 15 Market Hill, Cambridge CB2 3LW.

Salopia Saloon Coaches Ltd., Green End, Whitchurch, Salop.

Silcox Motor Coach Co. Ltd., 15–19 Water Street, Pembroke Dock, Pembs.

Smith's Luxury Coaches (Reading) Ltd., Queens Road, Reading, Berks.

Smith's Tours (Wigan) Ltd., 70 Market Street, Wigan, Lancs.

Votier Holdings Ltd., 1 Vulcan Road, Norwich NOR 89N.

Wessex Coaches Ltd., 73 Whiteladies Road, Clifton, Bristol 8.

Yelloway Motor Services Ltd., Weir Street, Rochdale, Lancs.

IRELAND, ISLE OF MAN AND CHANNEL ISLANDS

Guernsey Motors Ltd., Picquet House, St Peter Port, Guernsey.

Guernsey Railway Company, The, Picquet House, St Peter Port, Guernsey.

Isle of Man Road Services Ltd., PO Box 30, Station Buildings, Douglas,
  Isle of Man.

Jersey Motor Transport Co., Ltd., 2–4 Caledonian Place, Weighbridge,
  St Helier, Jersey.

Londonderry & Lough Swilly Railway Company, Pennyburn,
  Londonderry, N. Ireland.

*There are hundreds more smaller firms throughout the British Isles. You may like
to make your own list. How many of them can you find that run a public bus
service?*

Glossary

CERTIFICATE OF FITNESS Document certifying that the bus or coach named in it complies with the regulations as to its construction and maintenance.

CERTIFYING OFFICER Official of the Ministry of Transport responsible for the issue of Certificates of Fitness and having power to suspend or revoke them where vehicles cease to comply with the regulations.

CHAR-A-BANC Type of vehicle (long obsolete and never now seen) with rows of seats entered from each side, and no gangway. Plural (despite the pundits) is 'char-a-bancs', *not* 'chars-a-banc'.

CHART ROOM Control centre (for a company or a coach station) for allocating passengers to coaches and co-ordinating seats booked with capacity provided.

CHASSIS The underframe of a bus or coach, carrying the *engine* and *body*. Dispensed with in the case of *integral* construction.

CONTRACT A 'contract carriage' is one of the three legal sub-divisions of the *Public Service Vehicle*. The term is more often used to define a type of service operated under contract (instead of being open to the public at separate fares): e.g. 'works contract', 'school contract'.

DEAD WORKING Regular empty journey made to get the vehicle into position for its next operation, or to return it to depot. Sometimes 'light working', as in railway practice.

DEPOT A bus garage. Normally used only of garages providing maintenance facilities and staff. See *outstation*.

DUPLICATE A second or subsequent bus running on an advertised timing, or within five minutes before or after it. Often called a *relief* and sometimes (especially in Birmingham) a 'service extra'.

EXPRESS An 'express carriage' is another of the three legal sub-divisions of the *Public Service Vehicle*. The term 'express service' has a special legal meaning, of diminishing importance; more generally, it applies to a long distance coach service on which seats are booked in advance.

FLEET NAME The title painted on the side of a bus or coach, or on the rear, or both. It may be the operator's name, or it may be a special title. Its place is sometimes taken by a badge or a coat of arms.

GOODWILL When a business is sold, the buyer will pay a price higher than the actual value of the assets, and the difference represents the 'goodwill', or the loyalty of the customers to an established business.

INTEGRAL CONSTRUCTION In some buses and coaches, the body is specially strengthened so as to carry the engine and wheel assemblies, thus doing away with the need for a separate *chassis*. The practice is more common on the continent and in America than it is in Britain.

LEGAL LETTERING The official trading title of the owner of the vehicle, written in letters one inch high, must legally appear on the near side.

LIVERY The standard colour of a fleet. Some smaller operators do not go out of their way to re-paint second-hand vehicles, and may be said not to have a standard livery.

OUTSTATION Buses or coaches not kept at one of the main garages of the fleet are said to be 'outstationed'. This may mean they are kept in the garage of an associated company, or in a smaller garage belonging to their owner but lacking maintenance facilities or mechanical staff. This is sometimes called a 'dormy shed'.

PEAK That part of the day, week or year when demand is highest and all vehicles will be required to be on the road if at all possible, together with others hired from other operators in many cases.

PLATFORM STAFF Conductors.

PRIVATE Sign usually displayed on the destination blind of a bus or coach when it is either: 1, running empty (see *dead working*) or 2, operating as a *contract carriage*. When a coach is hired as a whole for an outing, the operation is known as a 'private hire' (US: 'charter').

PSV LICENCE Document required by law before a bus or coach can be used 'for hire or reward'.

PUBLIC SERVICE VEHICLE (PSV) The legal name for a bus or coach.

REGULATOR Official of a bus company whose job it is to see that services run smoothly by regulating them on the road. Some inspectors are regulators, others not.

RELIEF See *duplicate* and *service driver*.

ROAD SERVICE LICENCE Document authorising the operation of a bus or coach service, including excursions and extended tours.

ROAD STAFF Drivers, conductors and inspectors.

ROLLING STOCK The fleet of buses and coaches owned by an operator.

SERVICE DRIVER When a convoy of coaches is operated on one express service timing, the driver in charge is called the service driver, and his coach will sometimes be called the 'service car', to distinguish it from the remainder, which are called 'reliefs'.

STAGE A 'stage carriage' is the third of the three legal sub-divisions of the *Public Service Vehicle*, and the one most nearly approximate to the bus. The term 'stage service' has a special legal meaning, but is generally applied to any local public bus service. The word has a separate meaning in connection with the fare table, where each step is called a 'fare stage'.

TERRITORIAL COMPANIES The bus companies whose operations are limited as to area by agreements with their neighbours.

TRAFFIC COMMISSIONERS Licensing authorities set up by Act of Parliament to control the operation of buses and coaches, which they do by the issuing, suspending and revoking of *Public Service Vehicle Licences* and *Road Service Licences*. There are Traffic Commissioners for eleven 'traffic areas', and they are appointed by the Minister of Transport.

TRAFFIC COURTS Public sittings of the Traffic Commissioners, to decide upon applications for the grant or variation of *Road Service Licences*. They are not true 'courts', in the sense that the 'rules of court' do not generally apply to them.

Some useful books

For a more extensive study of the industry –
  William Lambden: *Bus and Coach Operation*. Iliffe, 1969.
For all sorts of information, stories, pictures, etc. –
  Gavin Booth (editor): *Bus Stop*. Ian Allan, 1969.
For the history of the industry from its beginning –
  John Hibbs: *The History of British Bus Services*. David & Charles, 1968.
For more about the vehicles themselves –
  David Kaye:
    Buses and Trolleybuses 1919 to 1945. Blandford, 1970.
    Buses and Trolleybuses from 1945. Blandford, 1968.
For a list of all current operators –
  The Little Red Book. Issued by Ian Allan annually.
For details of the nationalised companies –
  Who's Who in the NBC and STG. Issued by Travel & Transport
    occasionally.
For statistical and financial information –
  Annual Reports of: The National Bus Company.
                        The Scottish Transport Group.
                        The Traffic Commissioners.
  Passenger Transport in Great Britain (HMSO annually).

The monthly magazine for all interested in the industry is –
  Buses, published by Ian Allan.
The weekly trade papers, *Motor Transport* and *The Commercial Motor*, and
the monthly *Coaching Journal and Bus Review* will also be of interest.
The Chartered Institute of Transport Journal frequently includes articles about
the industry, while the Omnibus Society publishes a monthly magazine.

A note on timetables
The territorial companies issue complete timetables of their services, and
many of these include also details of other bus and coach operators and of
railway services in the area. Smaller operators differ a great deal in their

practice, and those in rural areas often assume that local passengers know their times by heart. The *Express Coach Guide* for Great Britain is published by the National Bus Company twice yearly and distributed by Ian Allan Ltd.; it includes details of all operators' services, subject to the limitations mentioned on page 32. Its American equivalent is *Russells Official National Motor Coach Guide*, which appears monthly.

Some useful addresses

Department of the Environment, 2 Marsham Street, London SW1.

The National Bus Company – 25 New Street Square, London EC4A 3AP.

The Scottish Transport Group – 114–116 George Street, Edinburgh.

The Association of Public Transport Operators (representing council transport departments and PTEs) – Friars House, Friars Place, Chelmsford, Essex.

The Public Road Transport Association (representing all the larger operators in England and Wales) – 172 Buckingham Palace Road, London S.W.2.

The Passenger Vehicle Operators Association (representing the independent operators) – 12 Emerald Street, London WC1N 3QE.

The Scottish Road Passenger Transport Association (representing the larger operators in Scotland) – 14 Queen Street, Edinburgh EH2 1JL.

The Chartered Institute of Transport (the professional body for all who work in transport management) – 80 Portland Place, London W1N 4DP.

The Institute of Road Transport Engineers, 1 Cromwell Place, London SW1.

The Omnibus Society (the senior 'enthusiasts' association) – 103a Streatham Hill, London S.W.2.

The PSV Circle (the association for people interested in the vehicles) – 52 Old Park Ridings, London N21 2ES.